I0572532

Editor's Picks

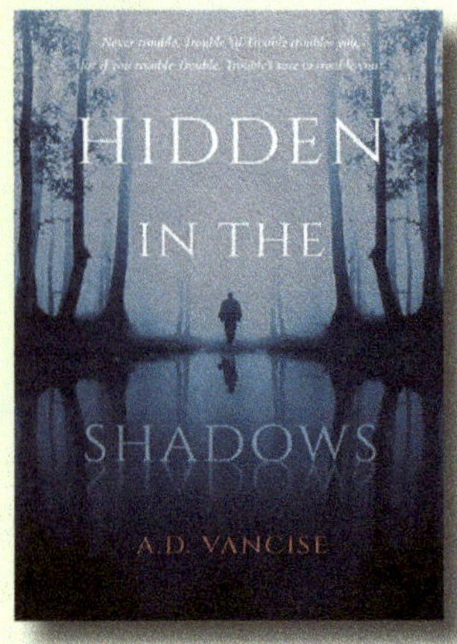

Hidden in the Shadows

A.D. VANCISE

A.D. Vancise masterfully crafts a suspenseful plot filled with atmospheric tension, captivating readers with its intrigue and richly layered narrative.

Paperback: £14.45

https://tinyurl.com/ysdt7crc

Skull's Vengeance

LINNEA TANNER

Linnea Tanner delivers a masterful blend of history, fantasy, and drama, creating an unforgettable tale with rich characters and intrigue.

Paperback: £15.37

https://tinyurl.com/k932uns9

Super Big Brother

DEANNA BUSSADORI

Super Big Brother is an enchanting tale that beautifully teaches children empathy and love, making it a must-read for families.

Paperback: £11.92

https://tinyurl.com/4yvrzukc

A Soul's Quest

KETAN KULKARNI

A beautifully crafted, soul-stirring fable that inspires self-discovery, inner strength, and living with purpose. Truly uplifting and timeless.

Paperback: £2.92

https://tinyurl.com/3z4tdjeb

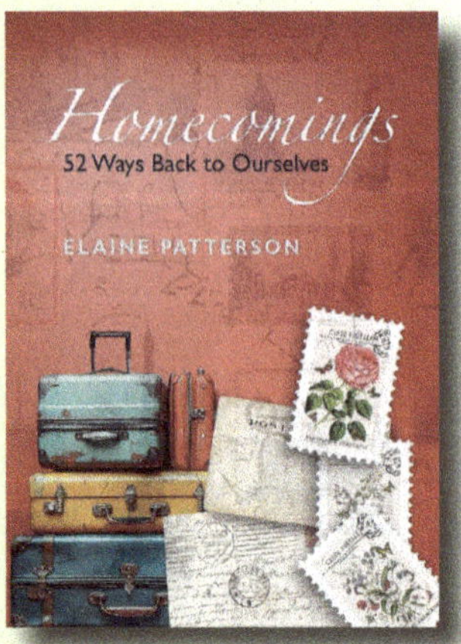

Homecomings

ELAINE PATTERSON

A beautifully written, soulful guide that gently leads you home to yourself with wisdom, grace, and heartfelt authenticity.

Paperback: £15.00

https://tinyurl.com/4rtaf7cp

My Place Among Them

J. STANION(GWEN MCPHAIL)

A powerful, beautifully written novel that captures resilience, identity, and the human cost of forced assimilation with depth and historical authenticity.

Kindle: £16.95

https://tinyurl.com/yc5hy89m

Boy Wander

JOBERT E. ABUEVA

Powerful, raw, and beautifully written—Boy Wander is a courageous journey of identity, resilience, and self-discovery that deeply resonates.

Paperback: £3.03

https://tinyurl.com/3kcanmya

The Spire

SHAUN GOLDSMITH

The Spire is a masterfully crafted thriller, combining intrigue, emotional depth, and unexpected twists that keep readers completely engrossed. Highly recommended!

Paperback: £12.23

https://tinyurl.com/a4xkzzh9

Your Gateway to Endless Stories

Coming Full Circle

BUDD TITLOW

A powerful, thought-provoking novel that masterfully blends history, environmental awareness, and human resilience—both captivating and deeply inspiring.

Paperback: £9.47

https://tinyurl.com/muyewxnk

The Fifth Bride of Pharaoh

CATALINA DUBOIS

A beautifully written, emotionally gripping tale of love, sacrifice, and defiance set in a vividly immersive ancient Egyptian world. Captivating and unforgettable!

Kindle: £1.58

https://tinyurl.com/f2j49yns

Where Is Charlotte

MARK GORKIN

Joyful, vibrant, and deeply engaging, Where Is Charlotte? celebrates confidence, inclusivity, and adventure through playful storytelling and sing-a-long charm.

Kindle: £4.99

https://tinyurl.com/472cr3yw

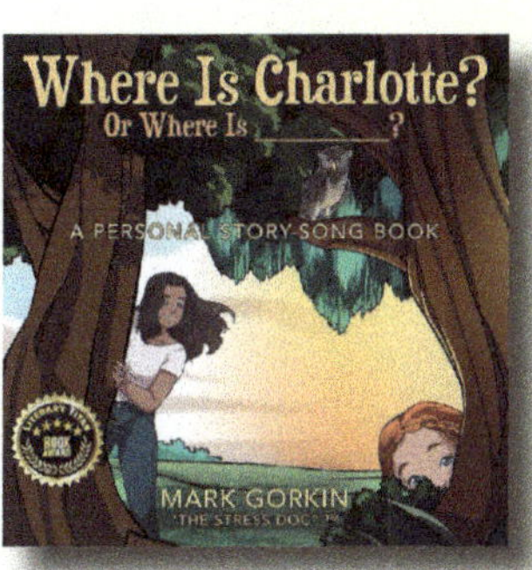

Ending Unnecessary Suffering

PETER RALSTON

Profound, insightful, and transformative—Ending Unnecessary Suffering offers a powerful guide to self-awareness, inner peace, and true mental freedom.

Paperback: £15.99

https://tinyurl.com/yx8tfb8k

The Big C^2

RUTH FEIN

Insightful, compassionate, and empowering—The Big C^2 is a must-read for anyone navigating chronic cancer. A beautifully written, invaluable resource.

Paperback: £13.53

https://tinyurl.com/4pka7c6v

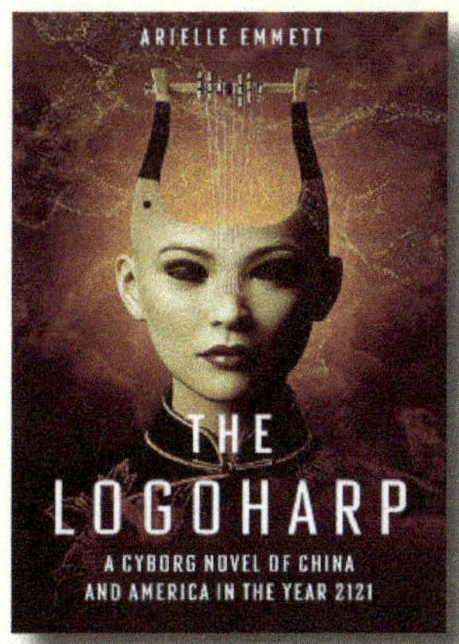

The Logoharp

ARİELLE EMMETT

Arielle Emmett delivers a bold, thought-provoking debut—brilliantly imaginative, emotionally resonant, and richly layered with futuristic and political depth.

Paperback: £14.17

https://tinyurl.com/mud2dta6

Wishes Are Free

DIANA MERCEDES HOWELL

A masterfully crafted tale that touches hearts, teaches empathy, and reminds us that friendship comes in unexpected, beautiful forms.

Kindle: £4.61

https://tinyurl.com/3rjenfmz

Henchmen

MATTHEW HUGHES

A gripping, witty fantasy adventure with rich world-building, engaging characters, and masterful storytelling—Hughes delivers intrigue, action, and unforgettable magic.

Paperback: £16.13

https://tinyurl.com/2wbe6ewn

VOICES OF LITERATURE

What's INSIDE

AUTHOR INTERVIEWS

What's INSIDE

What's INSIDE

Issue 54 -2025

EDITOR'S CHOICE

NOVEL • STORY • LITERATURE

EDITOR'S CHOICE highlights exceptional books, offering insightful reviews and recommendations to guide readers in discovering their next great read.

STAR INTERVIEW

Scan QR to read online or updated issue.

From the Editor

It is with great pleasure that we present to you the 54th issue of Reader's House, a celebration of literary excellence and the extraordinary authors who bring these stories to life. In this edition, we continue our tradition of showcasing works that not only entertain but also challenge, inspire, and resonate deeply with readers across the globe.

This issue is a vibrant tapestry of genres and voices, each offering a unique lens through which to view the world. From the gripping suspense of A.D. Vancise's *Hidden in the Shadows* to the rich historical fantasy of Linnea Tanner's *Skull's Vengeance*, these novels remind us of the power of storytelling to transport us to new realms and evoke profound emotions. We also shine a light on heartwarming tales like Deanna Bussadori's *Super Big Brother*, a touching narrative that teaches children the values of empathy and love, and Ketan Kulkarni's *A Soul's Quest*, a beautifully crafted fable that encourages self-discovery and inner strength.

In this issue's *Author Interviews* section, we're proud to introduce an incredible lineup of authors who shared their journeys, their perspectives, and their creative processes with us. Among them are Alisse Lee Goldenberg, Ashley Hasty, Ashley Weston, Autumn M. Birt, C. E. Clayton, Claudine Tinellis, Deepak Gupta, Dianne C. Braley, James Gilbert, Jaclyn Paul, Jane Doucet, Jannesy Deleon, Joan Epp, Joe Clark, Joe Kilgore, Joseph O'donoghue, Lea Harms, Liliana Tommasini, Raz Mihal, Shani T. Night, Stenetta Anthony, and Tina Sloan. Their insights offer a rare glimpse into the dedication, passion, and craftsmanship that define great writing, each conversation revealing the unique journey behind their remarkable works.

This issue also features thought-provoking reads like Peter Ralston's *Ending Unnecessary Suffering*, a transformative guide to self-awareness and mental freedom, and Shaun Goldsmith's *The Spire*, a masterfully crafted thriller that keeps readers on the edge of their seats. Whether you're drawn to the emotional depth of Elaine Patterson's *Homecomings* or the futuristic intrigue of Arielle Emmett's *The Logoharp*, there is something here to captivate every literary taste.

At Reader's House, we believe that books are more than just stories—they are mirrors reflecting our shared humanity, windows into unexplored worlds, and bridges connecting us to one another. We are honored to bring you this collection of works that embody the very best of contemporary literature.

As you turn the pages of this issue, we hope you find stories that move you, characters that stay with you, and insights that enrich your perspective. Thank you for joining us on this literary journey. Your passion for reading is what makes Reader's House a home for book lovers everywhere.

PUBLISHER: READER'S HOUSE MAGAZINE, A Subsidiary of NewYox Media Group. 200 Suite 134-146 Curtain Road, EC2A 3AR London, United Kingdom t: +44 79 3847 8420
editor@readershouse.co.uk II http://readershouse.co.uk II http://newyox.media
EDITORIAL: Anna Harlowe Editor-in-Chief, Dan Peters, Managing Editor, Ben Alan, Art Editor, Z. Robers , Content Editor.
CONTRIBUTORS Claudine D. Reyes, Andrea Piacquadio, Adrian T. Cheng, Donna Schim, Jon Allo, Tim Halloran, Oleg Magni, Amir SeilSepour, Bill Youngblood, Jetty Stutzman, Jimmy Choo, Peter Filinovich.

From Myth to Manuscript: The Stories Behind the Stories

Alisse Lee Goldenberg discusses her passion for folklore, character-driven storytelling, and balancing writing with family life. She reflects on her acclaimed series, collaborations, and the magic of theatre and screenwriting.

ALISSE LEE GOLDENBERG

WEAVES MAGIC AND MYTHOLOGY INTO CAPTIVATING STORIES ACROSS GENRES

By Z. Roberts I London

"People say to write what you know, and this is very much what my life is filled with."

Alisse Lee Goldenberg is a literary force whose storytelling seamlessly blends mythology, history, and imagination. An award-winning author of Children's Literature, Horror, Young Adult Paranormal Romance, and Fantasy, she has captivated readers with her rich narratives and compelling characters. With celebrated series such as *The Sitnalta Series, The Children of Colonodona, The Dybbuk Scrolls, and The Bath Salts Journals* (co-authored with An Tran), Goldenberg masterfully crafts worlds that are both immersive and unforgettable.

Her background in Fine Arts and Education, coupled with a lifelong fascination with folklore, infuses her writing with depth and authenticity. Whether she is exploring the supernatural through the lens of Jewish mythology or delving into the trials of courageous protagonists, her work is marked by vivid storytelling and emotional resonance. Beyond novels, she has also made her mark in theatre and screenwriting, proving her versatility across creative mediums.

In this exclusive interview, Goldenberg shares insights into her creative process, the inspirations behind her beloved works, and the delicate balance of writing while raising a family. Her passion for storytelling is evident in every word, offering an inspiring glimpse into the mind of a writer dedicated to bringing powerful narratives to life.

What initially inspired you to write fantasy and folklore-based stories, and how has your background in Fine

Arts and Education influenced your storytelling?

I have always been interested in fantasy and folklore. I had the good fortune of living with my bubbie (grandmother) while growing up, and she was a wonderful storyteller. She filled my head with tall tales from her homeland of Poland, so while other little girls grew up with Little Red Riding Hood, and Cinderella, I learned about the dybbuks and the shretelech of her childhood.

My degree is in Fine Arts Cultural Studies, so I had a lot of leeway in what I took, so I did courses in everything from Children's Literature to Apocalyptic Science Fiction, to Horror Films. Afterwards, Education made the most sense to me, as I loved reading and learning about what children love to read and learn about. Even today, most of what I read is what my kids hand me saying that I have to try it out. People say to write what you know, and this is very much what my life is filled with.

The Sitnalta Series features strong, determined characters facing incredible challenges. What is your approach to crafting compelling protagonists like Sitnalta?

For me, the most compelling protagonists are those that feel real. Even before I begin writing the plot, I create my characters. I get to know them, where they come from,

> Alisse Lee Goldenberg is a masterful storyteller, blending folklore, history, and imagination to create unforgettable characters and richly immersive worlds.

their entire biography. With Sitnalta, I got to know her from the day she was born. I looked at how she was raised, what she liked, and disliked, how her mind worked. In order for her to be a full-fledged person on the page, she had to become one in my mind. She had to have flaws, have heart, and feel like someone I could sit down and have a conversation with. When she was all of this, then I could write her story; because then I knew how she would react honestly in any given situation.

As a co-author of The Bath Salts Journals, how do you navigate the collaborative writing process with An Tran?

Writing with An Tran is almost ridiculously easy. She and I met when we were both teenagers doing a summer English programme in Oxford, and she's been one of my very best friends since. When I approached her, I didn't even know if she was interested in writing, but she also seemed like the most natural fit for this story. Knowing her love and respect for the zombie genre, I asked if she was interested. Her response was quick, enthusiastic, and slightly obscene. In other words, perfect for the project. Navigating working with her was simple. We crafted a rough sketch of where the story was going, and then each went our separate ways sending each other pages and mock diary entries as they were done. We've been workshopping a couple of other ideas since then. We'll see what happens.

Your works span multiple genres, from horror to children's literature. How do you adjust your writing style depending on the audience and genre?

I think that my writing style is consistent throughout. What I need to watch is the level of language I use. Certain words and phrases can be acceptable for a gory adult zombie story, but I need to be conscious about how they won't fly in a middle grade sports novel. But no matter what age range or genre I'm writing for, it's always character first and building the story around the hero.

Many of your books incorporate elements of mythology and folklore. Are there any specific legends or cultural stories that have heavily influenced your writing?

I'd say that a lot of my writing is influenced by the lasting mark my bubbie left on my life. She was a Holocaust survivor from Poland, and her stories of her childhood, and of the people she lost, how she coped with that and didn't just survive, but thrive has inspired much of what I do. Throughout my writing, there is a lot of that. I look at how loss and grief can be transformative. I look at the folklore she was raised with and raised me on. Specifically, she talked a lot about her own superstitions and belief in dybbuks. What to do to avoid their whims, and their possession. This is quite apparent in my Dybbuk Scrolls Trilogy.

Beyond books, you've also worked on screenplays and plays. How does writing for the stage or screen differ from writing novels, and do you have a preference?

I love theatre. I love the ability to see your words brought to life, and to hear the crowds react in real time. There is no rush quite like that. The frustrating thing is trimming the prose to make a script. Novels rely so much on description, and you get to write out what everyone is thinking, if that's your wish. There is no limit to what you can put on the page in a novel compared to a stage or screenplay. I sometimes find the limitations difficult to manoeuvre. So, when it comes to writing, I will tend to favour books.

What advice would you give to aspiring authors who are trying to balance writing with other responsibilities, such as family and career?

Don't beat yourself up over what you can accomplish within the given hours of the day. When it comes to balancing family and writing, I will always allow family to win out. My word documents will always wait for the kids to be asleep or at school. Kids are not so patient. I started my writing journey when my triplets were born. I like to joke that there was nothing good on t.v. at 3:00 a.m. (before the days of streaming). And so, I would write between feeds and diapers. Now, I write when they're at school, or asleep at night. I will never begrudge them the time they ask for during

> Twelve-year-old Sophie moves from Calgary to Stratford and struggles with homesickness. Her new house, though charming, holds secrets. When a mysterious girl appears in the garden, Sophie suspects the home is haunted. *The Ghost in the Garden* is a heartwarming, spooky tale of change, courage, and discovery.

Lessons in Writing, Self-Publishing, and Creativity

Autumn M. Birt discusses her journey from debuting Born of Water to mastering world-building, balancing multiple genres, and embracing travel-inspired storytelling, while offering invaluable advice for aspiring authors navigating self-publishing.

"Readers often say my worlds feel real, and that's because I write as if I'm standing there myself."

AUTUMN M. BIRT

CRAFTS FANTASTICAL WORLDS FILLED WITH MAGIC, ADVENTURE, AND GRIT

By Dan Peters I London

Autumn M. Birt is an award-winning and bestselling author who masterfully blends epic fantasy with immersive world-building. With over 20 novels to her name, she has captivated readers with intricate fantasy landscapes, dystopian thrillers, and even real-world adventures. Whether crafting elemental magic in Myrrah or navigating the emotional depths of war-torn futures, Birt brings a richness to her storytelling that stems from her own explorations across the globe.

In this exclusive interview for *Reader's House Magazine*, she shares the inspirations behind her fantasy realms, the challenges of debuting with *Born of Water*, and the lessons she's learned from a life spent travelling, writing, and embracing the unexpected.

What inspired you to create the world of Myrrah and its elemental magic system?

In the early 2000s, I had a story in my head about a professional woman—secretly a water elemental—who notices a girl with strange magic potential at a conference. But the idea stalled. Around the same time, the office where I worked had a massive Mediterranean painting—red cliffs, crashing waves, a brilliant sun, an endless sky. One day, I realized it held all the elements, and I wondered—what if my heroine lived there? That was the day Myrrah was born, along with Niri and Ria, the characters who would bring it to life.

What was the biggest challenge in writing Born of Water, and how did you overcome it?

The biggest challenge? It became my debut novel. Despite having a BA in English, I had a lot to learn about novel writing. I took adult education classes, wrote, rewrote, and rewrote again—including printing out the entire book and rearranging chapters on my living room floor. It was a process, but I stuck with it, publishing Born of Water in 2012.

Since then, I've grown tremendously as a writer, but this book remains a reader favorite, even winning reader awards as recently as 2020!

How do you balance writing across multiple genres, from epic fantasy to dystopian thrillers?

I read across multiple genres, so writing in them feels natural—like switching between different book series. I find it refreshing to go from a magic-filled epic fantasy to a gritty, fast-paced thriller.

But genre is just the surface layer. No matter what I write, I stay true to what defines my stories—deep, complex characters with a lot of grit who have big problems to solve in a fast paced style. And I always try to include themes of friendship and love, because I think those are important in the world and our lives.

Autumn M. Birt is a master storyteller whose immersive worlds, rich characters, and thrilling adventures captivate readers and ignite the imagination.

Your love for travel is evident—how has your nomadic lifestyle influenced your storytelling?

I think traveling has had a two-fold effect on my story telling.

The first is that I think my love of discovering new places—being overwhelmed by amazing scenery, smells, or tastes—bleeds into my writing. Readers often say my worlds feel real, and that's because I write as if I'm standing there myself.

And the second is it makes some of the fantasy travel a little less "fantasy." I have to admit I roll my eyes to read stories with people walking an aching number of miles in a day with absolutely no gear, catching dinner, and the weather is great. Just nope. My stories have mud, biting insects, plants that might eat you, days that you are thirsty, and you have to carry your tent—unless you have a pack animal... like a dragon.

Do you have a favourite character from any of your books, and if so, why?

I do love many of my characters and often when I'm writing a series, there is an absolute favorite there. But, looking back, the one that I still really love is Captain Jared Vries from Friends of my Enemy.

This is a dark, deeply emotional dystopian series that is often referred to as "Jane Austen meets WWIII." And Jared... is just so darn flippantly himself. He is the sort of character that has a comeback so witty even enemies have to laugh. And he is loyal, skilled enough to survive a futuristic wasteland, and is just the sort of bloke you'd want as a best friend.

I think that is why I love him. I'm so glad he popped into my mind, helped me write the series, and has stayed on as a sort of"good" guardian angel with a sarcastic streak.

How do you approach world-building to make your settings feel immersive and believable?

There's a science to world-building... and maybe an art to it, too.

To me, the true essence of making a fantastical place real is to create ecosystems—probably because I have a degree in ecology! If you can design a habitat that has evolved in a landscape, understand how a human-like culture would live there, add in their habits, beliefs, clothes, houses, you can make it feel real.

The hard part, really, is creating this immense knowledge base in your mind and not dumping it on a reader. Every reader should have the opportunity to explore through the eyes of the characters. Plus, there should be enough gaps, they get to add in their imagination as well. It takes a lot of work, but it is so much fun to write and share worlds with readers.

What advice would you give to aspiring authors trying to navigate self-publishing and marketing?

The first would be when you are writing your first book, don't rush it. Take the time to learn to write well, get help, get feedback, expect to have to rewrite it. It takes time to learn the ropes and if you go into it thinking you'll be great on your first draft, you are going to face disappointment. Instead, embrace the learning, love the journey, make friends along the way, and you'll come out with an amazing book, some wonderful supporters, and a passion to write.

The second would be you will have to market, indie or traditionally published author, but you can figure out what that looks like for you. Maybe you'll just want to run paid ads. Maybe you'll share your writing journey on social media. Perhaps you'll just post pins of characters. The important thing is to find a way of marketing you enjoy and that connects you with readers who will enjoy what you write. There are a million ways of making that happen.

In *Rule of Fire*, Niri, Ty, and Ria flee the Temple of Dust, pursued by the Church of Four Orders. As Ria struggles to control her forbidden magic, they ally with Khodan, a former weapon of the Church. Meanwhile, the vengeful Fire Elemental, Sinika, seeks escape, threatening their survival.

From Fantasy to Cyberpunk Futures

C. E. Clayton discusses her unique fusion of fantasy and cyberpunk, character development, horror elements, world-building methods, and how her academic background and life experiences shape her immersive storytelling.

C. E. CLAYTON

EXPLORING MAGIC, MACHINES, AND MEANING

"Good and bad communication, and interpersonal relationship skills played a huge part to the storytelling."

By Z. Roberts I London

C. E. Clayton is a name that fans of genre fiction should already have on their radar. With a rich bibliography spanning young adult fantasy, cyberpunk thrillers, and unsettling horror shorts, Clayton is not just a versatile storyteller—she's a genre-bender with a knack for world-building that feels both immersive and refreshingly original. Her work explores the intersections of magic and machine, love and survival, identity and destiny, often through complex protagonists navigating layered, vividly imagined worlds.

In this interview with *Reader's House Magazine*, Clayton opens up about her inspirations, from graphic novels and sci-fi epics to the realities of city life and academic studies in communication. She shares insight into her writing process, her character development arcs, and the delicate art of blending horror into fantasy. Whether you're already a devoted reader of *The Monster of Selkirk* or just discovering the technomagic intrigue of her *Eerden* novels, Clayton's passion for storytelling shines through every word.

What inspired you to blend cyberpunk elements with magic in your Eerden novels, such as 'Resistor'?

I was heavily inspired by the creatures, technology, and space travel in the graphic novel "Saga", the cyberpunk visuals and the morally questionable use of technology in "Altered Carbon", and the seamless blending of magic and technology in "Arcane". At the core of all these pieces of media, magic and technology hold hands. A futuristic world that still holds on to it's glittering wonder thanks to magic? I just find that too inspiring to ignore!

How did your background in communication management influence your storytelling approach in 'Encryption of the Heart'?

In a character driven romance like "Encryption of the Heart", good and bad communication, and interpersonal relationship skills played a huge part to the storytelling. During my coursework, I learned about the verbal and nonverbal forms of communication people use to convey ideas, feelings, and important information both in business and in their lives. Communication management focuses on understanding how people communicate, the tools they use to communicate with, and the intricacies of interpersonal relationships, both platonic and romantic. I took that understanding and applied it to two very different people with very different understandings of their situation. Which created both tension, and romance as the characters better navigated their interpersonal relationships.

Can you discuss the evolution of Tallis's character throughout 'The Monster of Selkirk' series?

Tallis is my character that most closely follows the heroes' journey. She occupies a unique space as a twist on the "chosen one" trope. At first, she doesn't fit in anywhere, and is unwanted by her adopted father. She had to learn what she's capable of, and when she discovers what that is, balancing the good person she is deep down with the terrible things she could do. She discovers her strength, then her control, and then chooses who she wants to be rather than what the prophecy dictates. It was a really fun evolution to explore because she goes from this lonely girl, to being told she's this monster everyone should fear, suffers due to others choices, and rather than embracing her destiny to take revenge on those who made her life miserable, she chooses to save them and become a hero instead.

> C. E. Clayton is a master of crafting imaginative, genre-blending stories filled with rich worlds, emotional depth, and unforgettable characters.

What challenges did you face when integrating horror elements into your fantasy narratives?

The biggest challenge is making sure those horror elements don't overshadow the story. I add just enough of a creepy factor to a scene to add that sense of menace and danger for the main characters without the story veering into a cryptid type horror novel. To achieve that balance, I make sure those horror elements are few and far in between, just enough for atmosphere, and not enough for the monsters to steal the scene away from the plot or main characters.

How did your personal experiences shape the world-building in your recent works?

I was born and raised a city girl. I know what it's like to live in a relatively small place crammed with people. I've seen the poverty and wealth stacked on top of each other, the crime that buts up against these glitzy restaurants and stores. I honestly love living in a city, but those zebra stripe extremes you get people and business wise when living in a city really inspired me.

What role does your involvement in the book community play in your writing process?

It helps me keep track of trends. The book community is very vocal about the kinds of characters, tropes and perspectives that they want to read about. Even if what they crave is a story I can't tell, it lets me keep a mental tab open on what tropes and vibes I might include.

How do you balance writing complex characters with maintaining engaging plotlines in your novels?

World building. By crafting the world first, it alters how characters interact with not just other characters, but the situation—and therefore makes the plot more engaging with very grounded conflict. For example, in my Eerden novels, that world includes a sentient robotic race. One of my characters has a deep prejudice against those types of robots. So, whenever they travel to a place in the world where those sentient robots are, it alters how she behaves and responds, and how other characters respond to her in turn. The story still moves forward, but the tension from the character elevates the plotline, and also allows me to create complex characters that are very natural in that world and story.

What advice would you give to aspiring authors aiming to create immersive fantasy worlds?

Create a world bible where you lay out everything about your world free of your characters. How your world functions will shape how your characters behave and respond to challenges. Figure out the topography, religion, government, language, what technology people have, what resources etc., and keep that all separate from whatever you use to build your characters. Most fantasy worlds will span several books, so having something easy to go back to and look up details has been a life saver for me as my books have morphed into a shared universe. I personally love using World Anvil for my world bible and have used it for years now.

Encryption of the Heart follows Olline Tavos, a brilliant software engineer with earth magic, who escapes heartbreak through a remote job—only to uncover a dangerous conspiracy. Forced to team up with a mysterious man, she must protect her magic, freedom, and heart in this tech-meets-magic romantic adventure.

Unlocking Potential Through Purpose, Communication and Leadership

Deepak Gupta, with decades of global leadership experience, presents a powerful blueprint to help individuals overcome invisible barriers and achieve lasting success.

DEEPAK GUPTA

SHARES THE SECRETS BEHIND HIS TRANSFORMATIONAL GUIDE TO SUCCESS

as told to Dan Peters

"We are too conscious about what others may think and say... this compromises our potential and performance."

Deepak Gupta is an extraordinary thinker, a seasoned leader, and an inspiring author who has spent over five decades shaping lives and careers across the globe. His remarkable journey, spanning three decades at the helm of various roles at Procter & Gamble in multiple countries, has fuelled his passion for empowering individuals to break through their limitations and unlock their true potential. Deepak has transformed his unparalleled professional experience into an enlightening body of work with his book, *Success is a Choice*. This compelling guide lays out the principles and skills essential for success, providing a transformative blueprint that resonates with readers from all walks of life.

In *Success is a Choice*, Deepak Gupta shares profound insights that demystify the elusive qualities required to excel both professionally and personally. Through his deeply relatable narrative and practical wisdom, he tackles key barriers to success, such as underdeveloped communication skills and self-imposed mental limitations, and helps readers focus on intentional actions. By blending his wealth of corporate experience with spiritual and sociological principles, Deepak has crafted a work that not only guides but inspires. His vision of success as a journey rather than a destination, coupled with his focus on empathy, inclusion, and self-awareness, makes his book a must-read for anyone striving to reach their full potential.

We are truly honoured to feature this dynamic author in this issue of *Reader's House*. Join us as Deepak shares his personal journey, the insights behind *Success is a Choice*, and his invaluable advice for aspiring writers and leaders. This conversation promises to leave you both motivated and equipped to embark on your own path to greatness.

What inspired you to transition from a senior executive role to becoming an author?

I had set a target to leave corporate life before I turned 55, giving me sufficient active time to lead a life of my choice. I got the opportunity at 53. Apart from business startups, a key objective for me was to share my experiential learnings for benefit of others. This was my way of giving back to society.

I have seen numerous brilliant people struggle at work because they are unable to succeed beyond a certain point as they lack some inexplicable skills. Even more worryingly, these work frustrations were affecting their personal and family lives. I decided to distil my learning into a book to help these talented individuals. 'Success is a Choice' is my attempt to demystify these skills and illustrate how to develop them and reach your full potential.

A compelling guide packed with wisdom, empathy, and real-world insight from a seasoned leader turned author.

Can you share a key lesson you learned during your time at Procter & Gamble that influenced your approach to leadership?

There are a few, and I have delved into these at length in 'Success is a Choice'. I will call out two here:

First, Success isn't merely a destination -- it's a continuous journey fuelled by intentional choices and committed action. No one, other than the individual, can define and evaluate his/her success.

Second, individual brilliance, by itself, is not enough. A leader must engage and enable his/her team to gain their commitment. This can only be achieved through empathy and compassion; control suboptimizes individual as well as team potential and performance.

In your book 'Success is a Choice', you focus on the skills that lead to success. Which of these do you believe is most underdeveloped in individuals today?

Communication is one of the most important factors for individual success or failure, not only in professional but also in personal lives. Unfortunately, it is also the most underdeveloped skill in individuals today. Communication is often confused with the ability to converse or speak. Not many realize that effective communication is the art of using sight, sound, feel and thought to succinctly convey exactly what we want to share. Few quotes from 'Success is a Choice' :

"THOUGHT is the mind, and FEEL is the heart of effective communication; both are essential to enhance its efficacy and impact. 'Feel' creates the awareness and understanding and 'thought' brings coherence and mindfulness."

"Though intuitive that a thought is an essential first step, 'Think' is an oft-forgotten part of the communication cycle. This 'given' is often neglected and communication starts without 'Think', leading to either communication problems and misunderstandings, or ends up being ineffective."

How has your experience living and working in different countries shaped your perspective on leadership and success?

I was born and brought up in India, one of the most diverse countries in the world. Working for a global company gave me the opportunity to live in six culturally different countries and work closely with colleagues from more than twenty nationalities. This unparalleled exposure to different cultures and traditions gave me excellent insights into people psyche. It helped me create an inclusive environment that thrives on diversity and allows everyone to perform at their full potential.

I also realized and appreciated that despite the cultural diversity, the success skills are constant across the world. As a result, 'Success is a Choice' provides a blueprint and empowers global readers with a practical framework to elevate their professional and personal lives and achieve their goals.

What do you consider the most common mindset barriers that prevent people from reaching their full potential in the corporate world?

'We' ourselves, are our biggest barrier. We are too conscious about what others may think and say. Instead of laser-like focus on what really matters, we spend inordinate time on gaining others' approval; this compromises our potential and performance.

Could you discuss the role of spiritual and sociological teachings in shaping your views on success and personal growth?

Yes, it has impacted my outlook towards success. The concept of focusing on your actions rather than worrying about the result is ingrained in spirituality and is the bedrock principle for happiness.

I am a firm believer that only our actions are in our control, not their consequence; the result is an outcome of how well we perform our actions, duties and responsibilities. Fretting over Results, which are not in our control, causes undue anxiousness, stress, and frustration and in fact compromises what is in our control -- our designated actions, taking us further away from success.

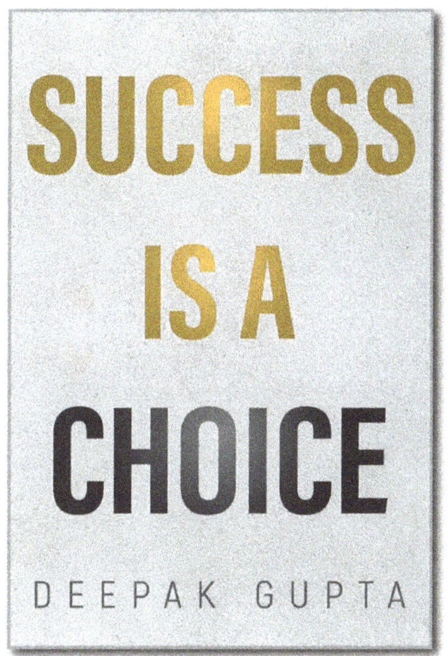

Success is a Choice by Deepak Gupta is a self-help book set in a fictional corporate world. It follows executive Dan Webber's journey to success through mentorship, revealing how mindset shifts, spiritual insights, and practical strategies can overcome stagnation and empower individuals to choose and achieve lasting success.

What advice would you give to other authors who aspire to write self-help books based on their professional experiences?

Be courageous and do not hesitate to share your professional and personal experiences. Even seemingly simple learnings can be invaluable for young people in quest for knowledge and wisdom. Our experiences can help them avoid the mistakes that we made in our lives. A common theme in the feedback on my book is, "I wish 'Success is a Choice' was available to me when I started my career."

The Power of Storytelling in Overcoming Trauma

Dianne C. Braley discusses her journey from nursing to writing, the inspiration behind her novels, the impact of addiction, and the emotional depth of her storytelling, set against the backdrop of Martha's Vineyard.

DIANNE C. BRALEY

WEAVES GRIT, RESILIENCE, AND HEART INTO STORIES THAT ECHO LONG AFTER THE LAST PAGE

"Healing isn't linear, and neither is the experience of loving someone who is battling addiction."

By Ben Alan I London

Dianne C. Braley is a writer of remarkable depth, one who weaves personal history into fiction with a raw and compelling honesty. Her work is as evocative as it is necessary, bringing to life the silent battles of addiction, the complexities of human relationships, and the enduring scars of trauma. With *The Silence in the Sound*, she has given readers an unforgettable novel—one that does not shy away from the painful truths of loving someone in the grip of addiction.

Beyond fiction, Braley's *Unheard Whispers* peels back the layers of childhood wounds in striking poetry, capturing moments of sorrow and survival with haunting precision. *The Summer Before* further solidifies her reputation as a fearless storyteller, tackling the emotional wreckage left in the wake of crime and betrayal. These works are not just stories; they are necessary conversations, shedding light on the unspoken struggles so many endure in silence.

A former nurse, Braley's career took an unexpected turn when she cared for Pulitzer Prize-winning author William Styron on Martha's Vineyard—a fateful encounter that reignited her passion for writing. The island, with its idyllic beauty and underlying tensions, has since become a recurring presence in her work, serving as both refuge and mirror to her characters' internal landscapes.

In this issue of *Reader's House*, Braley opens up about the deeply personal inspirations behind her books, her journey as a writer, and the enduring themes of love, pain, and redemption. Her words are unflinching yet hopeful, offering solace to those who see their own struggles reflected in her pages. We are honoured to present this conversation with a writer who does not just tell stories but gives voice to those who have long remained unheard.

How did your personal experiences growing up in an environment affected by alcoholism influence the themes and characters in your novel The Silence in the Sound?

I grew up in an alcoholic home with a father who struggled with addiction, and like so many who come from that world, I thought I had escaped it—only to run right back into it. When you grow up surrounded by something, it becomes familiar, even when it's painful. Without realizing it, I gravitated toward what I knew. I fell in love with someone who mirrored the chaos I thought I had left behind.

I ended up on Martha's Vineyard, a place that seemed so far removed from my past. It was beautiful, pristine, an island where people escape for a perfect summer, where the horrors of addiction and dysfunction shouldn't exist. But they exist everywhere. That's something I had to learn the hard way.

This realization became the foundation of The Silence in the Sound. My protagonist, like me, believes she has outrun the ghosts of her past, only to find them in a different form, in a different place. The novel explores how addiction weaves itself into our lives, how love and pain become tangled, and how we sometimes have to break completely before we can truly escape.

Can you share how your time caring for a Pulitzer Prize-winning novelist on Martha's Vineyard reignited your passion for writing and inspired your literary career?

Caring for William Styron was a transformative experience. Here I was, a nurse tending to this literary giant, and instead of feeling like an outsider in his world, I felt drawn to it—like something in me had been waiting for permission to return to writing. Being on Martha's Vineyard, surrounded by so much history and artistic energy, only amplified that. Our conversations, his encouragement, and simply being in his presence reignited a fire in me that I had nearly let burn out. It made me realize that writing wasn't just a dream I'd abandoned but something I was meant to do.

> Dianne C. Braley's storytelling is fearless, deeply moving, and profoundly honest, illuminating the struggles of addiction, trauma, and human resilience with grace.

The Summer Before delves into the complexities of friendship and trauma. What inspired you to explore these themes, and how did you approach writing about such sensitive subjects?

The Summer Before was inspired by a real trial that deeply impacted my life. I wanted to bring light to secondary victims—the family and friends of the perpetrator—who often become voiceless and shunned. While the primary victim should always be the main focus, we cannot ignore the collateral damage these crimes leave behind. The more we see these crimes brought to light, the more we must have open dialogue about the ripple effects they cause.

These secondary victims, who never asked for their lives to be turned upside down, are often left to navigate shame, guilt, and isolation. I wanted to tell a story that not only acknowledged their suffering but also showed how difficult it is to reconcile love for someone who has done the unthinkable. To ensure I handled this topic with the care it deserves, I conducted extensive research, listening to the testimonies of both primary and secondary victims.

At its core, The Summer Before is also a story about friendship—the kind that shapes, saves, and sometimes shatters us. Childhood friendships are often our first real love stories, yet we rarely explore them with the same depth as romantic relationships. Maddie and Summer's bond is intense, complicated, and tested in ways neither could have imagined. Trauma has a way of exposing the cracks in relationships, and I wanted to explore what happens when the person you trusted most becomes part of your deepest pain. The more we talk about this, the less power silence has in allowing these crimes to hide in the shadows.

Your poetry collection Unheard Whispers addresses the challenges of growing up in an alcoholic home. What motivated you to express these experiences through poetry, and how does this medium differ from your prose work?

Poetry strips away everything but the raw emotion. While my novels allow me to build a world around my experiences, poetry lets me distill them down to their essence. Unheard Whispers was my way of capturing those fleeting, haunting moments of childhood—the whispered arguments, the unspoken apologies, the love wrapped in chaos. It's deeply personal, yet I think it resonates with so many who have lived in similar circumstances.

As a registered nurse, how has your medical background influenced your storytelling, particularly in portraying characters' emotional and physical struggles?

Nursing has given me a front-row seat to humanity at its most vulnerable. It's impossible not to carry those experiences into my writing. I understand trauma—not just emotionally, but physically. I know what grief looks like in a person's posture, how fear manifests in small, unconscious movements. That depth of understanding helps me create characters that feel real, whether they're fighting inner demons or dealing with physical hardship.

Martha's Vineyard serves as a significant setting in your work. What draws you to this location, and how does it enhance the narratives you create?

Martha's Vineyard is more than just a setting—it's a character in itself. There's a haunting beauty to the island, a mix of privilege and isolation, history and hidden stories. I lived there for a time and still return often. It's a place that can feel both like an escape and a trap, which made it the perfect backdrop for my stories. The island's charm and contradictions reflect so much of what my characters struggle with—longing, loss, and the push-and-pull between past and present.

It's also a place where secrets can be both deeply buried and impossible to hide. There's something about an island that heightens emotions—its isolation magnifies struggles, and the ever-present ocean serves as both a sanctuary and a force of reckoning. That duality speaks to the themes in my work. It's a place where people reinvent themselves, but also where the past has a way of resurfacing. For my characters, the island represents both the illusion of escape and the inescapable truths they must face.

Martha's Vineyard is more than just a setting—it's a character in itself. There's a haunting beauty to the island, a mix of privilege and isolation, history and hidden stories. I lived there for a time and still return often. It's a place that can feel both like an escape and a trap, which made it the perfect backdrop for my stories. The island's charm and contradictions reflect so much of what my characters struggle with—longing, loss, and the push-and-pull between past and present.

Your writing often addresses the impact of addiction on families. What message do you hope readers take away regarding this issue?

Addiction isn't just about the addict—it's about everyone who loves them, too. It's easy to paint addiction in black and white, but the reality is filled with shades of gray. I hope readers walk away with a deeper understanding of that complexity—the guilt, the hope, the anger, and the love that exist simultaneously. More than anything, I want people to feel

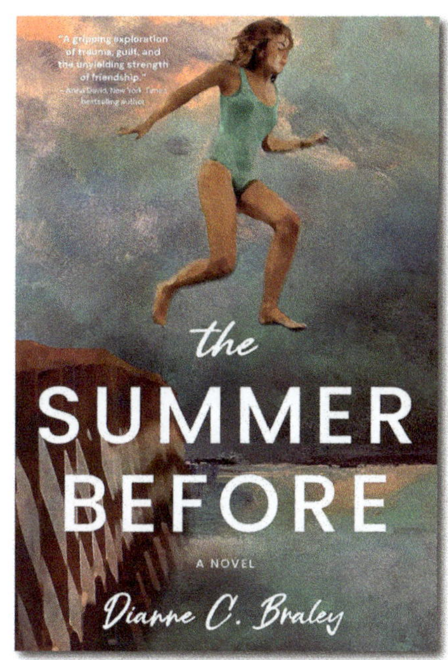

> Madeline and Summer share a deep bond, but Summer's hidden trauma shatters their lives. Years after the trial that divided her family, Madeline struggles with guilt and suicidal thoughts. To heal, she must confront her past, family, and painful truths in this gripping story of trauma, betrayal, and resilience.

seen, to know they're not alone in their experiences.

I also want to challenge the stigma surrounding addiction. Too often, society treats addiction as a moral failing rather than the disease that it is. This not only harms those who struggle with it but also alienates the people who love them. Families of addicts are often left to navigate immense emotional turmoil in silence, fearing judgment or blame. I want my stories to create a space for those conversations—to shed light on the pain, but also on the resilience and love that endure despite it. Healing isn't linear, and neither is the experience of loving someone who is battling addiction.

Addiction isn't just about the addict—it's about everyone who loves them, too. It's easy to paint addiction in black and white, but the reality is filled with shades of gray. I hope readers walk away with a deeper understanding of that complexity—the guilt, the hope, the anger, and the love that exist simultaneously. More than anything, I want people to feel seen, to know they're not alone in their experiences.

What advice would you offer to aspiring authors who wish to draw from personal experiences to create compelling fiction?

Be honest, but also be kind—to yourself and your characters. Writing from personal experience can be cathartic, but it's important to step back and allow the story to breathe beyond your own pain. Give your characters autonomy. Let them surprise you. And remember, just because something happened to you doesn't mean you have to tell it exactly as it was. Fiction gives you the space to reshape and explore without being bound by reality.

The Art of Blending History and Imagination

James Gilbert, an acclaimed historian-turned-novelist, discusses his transition to fiction, the inspirations behind his Amanda Pennyworth Mystery Series, his global experiences, and how history shapes his compelling narratives.

JAMES GILBERT

A MASTERFUL STORYTELLER BRIDGING HISTORY AND FICTION

BY READER'S HOUSE STAFF

"Living abroad has empowered me to imagine environments and individuals outside my given world."

James Gilbert's name is synonymous with intellectual curiosity and masterful storytelling. With a career spanning academia and fiction, he has brought history to life in one form and crafted gripping narratives in another. As a distinguished Professor of American History at the University of Maryland, his scholarly contributions shaped discussions on twentieth-century culture. Yet, his restless pursuit of understanding the human experience ultimately led him to fiction, where he continues to explore the intricacies of identity, society, and mystery.

His Amanda Pennyworth Mystery Series is a testament to his ability to weave suspense with cultural insight, creating a protagonist who navigates diplomacy as deftly as she unravels crime. With *Murder at Amapas Beach*, Gilbert demonstrates the skill of a seasoned mystery writer, blending atmosphere, tension, and character development in a way that echoes the best of classic whodunits while offering something distinctly modern. Beyond his mysteries, his novels such as *The Legacy* and his short story collections immerse readers in richly drawn worlds, shaped by his deep understanding of history and human nature.

In this conversation, James Gilbert reflects on the journey from historian to novelist, the inspirations behind his intricate plots, and the way his global experiences inform his fiction. His words are as insightful as his books—offering wisdom for aspiring writers and an invitation to explore the stories he so expertly crafts.

How did your transition from a distinguished academic career in American cultural history to writing fiction influence your storytelling approach?

I was initially surprised to recognize that historical literature and fiction are so closely linked. Even if historians are bound by rules of objectivity, they are, in the first instance, also story-tellers and the inventors of plots. So I consider that my years as a historian to be a kind of apprenticeship for writing novels and short stories.

What inspired you to create the character of Amanda Pennyworth, the American consul and amateur sleuth in your mystery series?

Several years ago I served on the U.S. State Department's promotion panel. I met a number of Department diplomats and read hundreds of employee files, coming away with a good sense of what problems and opportunities faced members of the diplomatic corps. Based on my frequent trips to Puerto Vallarta, Mexico, I imagined what it might be like to be the sole American representative in a popular foreign tourist destination. So many opportunities for things to go wrong!

> James Gilbert's storytelling brilliance seamlessly merges history, mystery, and human complexity, captivating readers with his masterful prose and richly developed characters.

Could you share the process behind developing the plots for the Amanda Pennyworth mystery series, particularly in 'Murder at Amapas Beach'?

Like so many writers, the plots of my novels develop out of memories or references to my own experiences. During one of my visits to Puerto Vallarta, I went on a day trip to a nearby beach—in the company of a group of Americans. When I sat down to develop my novel, I thought this would be a perfect setting for a mystery: an isolated location and a limited group, one of whom would be the victim and another, the murderer. In a way, this closed circle was something like the traditional country house filled with suspects that Agatha Christie used as her staple. But, of course, I had to invent motives and characters. And then I decided to move the scene abruptly back to the United States to the home town of the American tourists in the second half of the book. And then stage another murder with the same suspects. And, of course, create a plausible reason for Amanda to be present.

In each of my Pennyworth novels, I have also tried to develop the character of Amanda, to let the reader know much more about her, her background, her relationships, and about how she went about solving the mysteries that confronted her—even as she had to face the ongoing, daily problems of serving as American consul.

Your short story collections often revolve around specific places and time periods with interconnected characters. How do you approach crafting these narrative?

Both of my short story collections reference places, or especially in the case of "Tales of Little Egypt," historical events and cultures that I know well, either from historical research or actual experience. Creating the stories, however, comes from imagining what it would be like to live in these situations. In this way, the setting creates possibilities for characters to come alive in the very special worlds where they exist.

In 'The Legacy', you delve into the complexities of the legal world. What motivated you to explore this setting, and how did your background inform this novel?

I grew up in a family situated in a world of lawyers and legality, although I never studied law myself. But I am sure that this background focused my attention on the two most important documents that describe any individual: a birth certificate and a will. The first defines where a person comes from and the second reveals what she or he has made of themselves—how they reach into the future to define their heritage. In the case of my novel, both documents disguise and then reveal secrets that shatter the relations of a troubled family and threaten the reputation of a law firm.

Having taught at various international institutions, how have your global experiences shaped the settings and themes in your fiction works?

Living abroad for a number of years and being immersed in foreign languages and cultures had been instrumental in my fiction. I think foremost, it has empowered me to imagine environments and individuals outside my given world. I suppose, too, in some instances, that I have borrowed people I have met and transformed them into characters in my novels and stories. But there is also, I believe, something amazingly enlightening—something that untethers the imagination, in confronting the unexpected which inevitably occurs when living in a culture that isn't your own.

Your historical writings, such as 'A Cycle of Outrage', examine societal reactions to cultural phenomena. How has this perspective influenced your fiction writing?

The most important idea I've drawn from history is to realize the power of culture to define a setting or template in which people act and events occur. In all of my fiction writing, I try to devote special attention to the plausibility of the atmosphere, the prevailing beliefs and moods, even the time periods, and the particularities of the locations and individuals who are my characters.

What advice would you offer to aspiring authors transitioning from academic writing to fiction storytelling?

Of course, my answer has to do with the particular academic field, and that, certainly has to be influential in how the author confronts fiction. But the simple and best advice I can give is find ways to use whatever knowledge and expertise has been gained in academics. Almost every discipline requires and values writing—good writing—and that can be a wonderful beginning. And from there, remember and rejoice in the freedom that fiction allows!

> Richard Collins, facing his impending death, gathers his three sons at their lakeside home to reveal his will. What he expects to be a solemn moment instead ignites turmoil, exposing deep-seated family tensions. As his wife and sons confront their legacy, long-standing conflicts and personal struggles come to light.

The Mastermind Behind Award-Winning Horror Novels

JOHN K. ADDIS

MEET THE AUTHOR WHO'S CAPTIVATING READERS WITH HAUNTING TALES AND UNFORGETTABLE CHARACTERS

as told to Dan Peters

In this interview, John K. Addis discusses his unique creative process, influences, and his journey as an independent author navigating the horror genre.

John K. Addis is a name that resonates with creativity, versatility, and an unrelenting passion for storytelling. A design and marketing professional by trade, Addis has carved a remarkable path across multiple artistic disciplines, from composing music and directing films to creating comic strips and performing in a rock band. Yet, it is his literary achievements that have truly captured the imagination of readers worldwide. His debut horror novel, The Eaton, not only became an Amazon and Audible bestseller but also garnered multiple awards, cementing his place as a master of the genre. Addis's ability to blend psychological depth with supernatural horror has drawn comparisons to the likes of Stephen King, though his meticulous approach to crafting endings sets him apart as a storyteller of unique vision.

In this exclusive interview, Addis offers a glimpse into the creative process behind his works, including his semi-autobiographical novel The Paper, which reimagines his childhood in Michigan with a supernatural twist. He also reflects on the challenges of transitioning from other creative fields to novel writing, his influences, and his decision to remain an independent author despite the success of The Eaton. With a new project on the horizon, revisiting the plot of his first attempted novel, Addis continues to prove that his creative well is far from running dry. It is a privilege to feature this extraordinary author in the pages of Reader's House, and we invite you to delve into his world of haunting tales, vivid characters, and boundless imagination.

A recent critic said your novels "blend psychological depth with supernatural horror." Why is this important to you?

As a genre, horror often carries the stereotype of having undeveloped characters, particularly in film, where frequent deaths leave little time to explore motivations and backstories. That's not to say I avoid genre archetypes altogether—I enjoy putting my spin on tropes like The Final Girl, The Cynical Skeptic, or The Doomed Couple. But novels provide time and space to let characters breathe and grow, making it far more impactful when supernatural events

Continued *on page 42*

"John K. Addis, the visionary author whose award-winning novels intertwine psychological complexity with supernatural horror, captivates readers worldwide.

Continued *from page 40*

John K. Addis masterfully weaves nostalgia and horror in *The Paper*, a gripping tale set in 1988. Through the eyes of seventh graders Jimmy and Dale, the story explores adolescence amid small-town mysteries and personal growth. The atmospheric blend of psychological depth and supernatural elements keeps readers hooked. An exceptional coming-of-age novel that resonates beyond its genre. Highly recommended!

unfold. Fear resonates with the reader more deeply when weird things happen to genuine, complicated people who are more than mere fodder for the plot.

How much of The Paper is based on your own childhood experiences in Michigan?

The Paper is a quasi-autobiographical tale from my time growing up in the small town of New Haven in the late 1980s. I really did publish a hometown newspaper at age 11, and I really did write articles about the creepy abandoned house at the end of our street, which all the neighborhood kids believed was haunted. In the novel, however, the house truly is haunted, and I imagine how this change might have impacted specific events and friendships during my coming-of-age years.

Can you share more about the creative process behind your debut novel, The Eaton?

It's a little embarrassing, but the core concept of The Eaton came from a vivid dream I had about being chased by a monster through an old, abandoned hotel. Initially, it wasn't meant to be a novel; it started as a weekly "serial" blog to entertain my friends and family. That's why each chapter ends with a twist or hook to encourage readers to "tune in next week"—a trick I borrowed from Charles Dickens.

After about ten weeks of posting in this way, I realized I wanted to refine the story and rework it into a proper novel. This meant drafting chapter outlines, creating blueprints and physical maps, and even using character tokens to track everyone's location in key scenes. I also did a lot of historical research into Victorian-era Eaton Rapids, Michigan, particularly for the chapters set in the past.

Was it always your intention to publish independently, or did you first try traditional publishing?

I considered submitting the first draft to agents and publishing houses, but I struggled to find anyone willing to take on horror from an unknown author. In the 1980s, there were over a hundred U.S. publishing houses specializing in genre fiction, but after the consolidation of the early 2000s, most were absorbed or shut down. Besides, although I knew that self-published novels rarely sell over 100 copies, I was surprised to learn that the average traditionally published novel only sells 500 to 1,500 copies in its first year, and I'd have to give up the rights to my intellectual property.

I decided to start my own imprint with the ambitious goal of selling 1,000 copies of The Eaton, which would be a rare feat for a self-published title. To my surprise, it sold over 10,000 copies in its first year. Traditional publishers took notice, but by then, I knew I wanted to remain independent.

What challenges did you face transitioning from other creative fields to writing novels?

Writing stories has always been my first creative love. I tried writing a full-length novel in college, The Vacancy, but only made it halfway through before switching to amateur filmmaking instead. Unlike other creative pursuits, novel writing requires a great deal of long-term discipline, which I didn't have in my teens or twenties—and, honestly, I barely have in my forties!

Are there any authors or works that have significantly influenced your storytelling approach?

My favorite storytellers, and therefore the most likely influences on my style, are Jeffrey Eugenides, David Mitchell, and Ray Bradbury. Many readers compare my writing to Stephen King, which I think is fair, and intentional. I've been a huge King fan since my teens and have read almost everything he's written. No one in our genre is in his league.

That said, my approach differs from King's, for better or for worse. He famously writes without planning his endings, letting the story unfold naturally. I, on the other hand, meticulously plan my endings first. As the saying goes, I believe a good ending should feel both "surprising yet inevitable," and for me, that requires knowing where I'm headed from the start.

> *"Fear resonates with the reader more deeply when weird things happen to genuine, complicated people."*

Are you currently working on anything new?

Yes! I've decided to revisit the plot of my first attempted novel, The Vacancy. I'll be starting from scratch since my writing skills have grown considerably since college, but I still believe the plot is strong and worth exploring.

The biggest challenge is finding time to write. Between running a 20-person design firm, taking Master's classes, serving on nonprofit boards, performing with the Black Barn Band, and trying to be a present father and husband, it's a lot to juggle. But as most writers will tell you, when a story takes root in your mind, it consumes your thoughts. It's like a nagging little demon that refuses to leave until you let it out, no matter how busy you are. In fact, I might have to start right now! "Susan was torn from her nightmare by the sound of a scream..."

John K. Addis is a remarkable storyteller whose rich imagination and psychological depth elevate the horror genre to new heights; he's truly a modern literary treasure.

John K. Addis proudly showcases his prestigious awards, including the 2024 Editor's Choice Award for Literary Excellence from Reader's House and recognition as a finalist in the American Advertising Awards.

JOHN K. ADDIS

Whether authoring a novel, creating short films, writing political articles, composing original songs, or crafting marketing copy for my clients, I have always been a storyteller. As a child, I filled up endless journals of short stories, and created countless hours of movies on my Fisher Price PXL-2000 camcorder. As an alleged grown-up, I've found ways of turning my love of storytelling into my career and hobbies. If you're into storytelling yourself, you may have seen one of my presentations on modern publishing, or if you're a fan, attended a book signing.

The Eaton was my first completed full-length novel, and I remain humbled at the overwhelming response and reception it received. It reaffirmed my desire and commitment to telling Michigan-based stories. I had, after all, created a variety of Michigan-themed projects before that, from my daily comic strip Studentangle which ran in Michigan State University's The State News, to writing and directing the cult local miniseries The Bells of Beaumont Tower, which Unspeakable Magazine described as "one hell of a story." (My first review!) I have always felt that Michigan is underrepresented in modern fiction, and I'd like to have at least a tiny part in changing that.

Until recently, I've resisted the urge to publish a writer's website, as I'm quite a bit overwhelmed with commitments. In addition to my day job owning and operating a design and marketing firm (Addis Enterprises) with 20 full-time creative professionals, I also play keys and occasional vocals in a mid-Michigan cover band (The Black Barn Band), serve as Lt. Governor of District 6 of the American Advertising Federation, am earning an MBA in Marketing, and still need to find time to travel with my wife and be goofy with my three creative, hysterical kids. I point these commitments out not to humblebrag or to expect sympathy, but as my response to repeated questions from family, friends, and fans about when I'm finally going to release Book X or Book Y that I've been teasing for ages. Be patient! Everything will get done eventually. Just, first I need to argue politics with a stranger online for an hour. (Squirrel!)

So if you're reading this, please know how much it means to me that you've sought me out. It's only fun being a storyteller if people actually enjoy the stories you're telling. I will be publishing at least five (!) projects over the next calendar year, and with any luck, one of them will be your favorite. And if not, well, I'll just have to keep trying.

A Canadian Author Turns Nature into Childhood Magic

Joan Epp, retired teacher and farmer, debuts a heartwarming children's book inspired by her granddaughter and the natural world around her.

"Weaving personal experiences into a dance of ideas that became my debut work was exhilarating!"

JOAN EPP

SHARES THE STORY BEHIND HER SNOWBOARDING SNOWMAN

BY READER'S HOUSE STAFF

Joan Epp is a literary gem whose journey to becoming a published author is as inspiring as the stories she writes. Hailing from the picturesque shores of Lake Erie in Ontario, Canada, Joan brings a unique tapestry of life experiences to her work, seamlessly weaving her roles as a teacher, farmer, artist, and grandmother into every word she pens. Her debut children's picture book, *Ice Cap,* is nothing short of enchanting—a modern twist on the beloved snowman tale that delights young readers and adults alike. With its universal message of friendship and gratitude and its distinctly Canadian heart, *Ice Cap* introduces us to a snowboarding snowman who has quickly captured imaginations far beyond the frosted landscapes of his origin.

As a storyteller, Joan is wonderfully connected to both the natural world and the boundless curiosity of her young readers. Her books carry the beauty and vibrancy of the flora and fauna near her home, while her own engaging presence as "Gramma Joan" invites children to see themselves as co-creators of stories. Joan doesn't just write for children—she inspires them, leading by example to show that stories can be born from everyday life, family connections, and even a spark of imagination from a four-year-old granddaughter.

In this interview, Joan shares insights into her creative process, the influence of her rich personal history, and the joyful journey that saw her scribbled dreams take flight as published works. Whether she's speaking about her love of nature, her passion for encouraging young storytellers, or her tenacity in overcoming challenges, Joan reminds us all that every story is a treasure waiting to be told. It was an honour to sit down with this remarkable author and celebrate the gift of storytelling she brings to the world.

How did your experiences as a teacher and farmer influence the creation of "Ice Cap," your debut children's book?

Weaving personal experiences into a dance of ideas that became my debut work was exhilarating! As a teacher, I wanted readers to decode and predict the text using rhyme, connect with the content, and infer meaning imbedded in the rich vocabulary of my story. The diversity of my students also had to be pictured in my story because children relate to books with characters who look like them. "Ice Cap" is Canadian but I feel there are no geo-political boundaries when writing for children. As a farmer I'm surrounded by resources. The husks from cornfields became dolls in my story. The grapevines from my fencerow became Ice Cap's heart of gold. We tend to order everything online but we could all learn from a modern-day Frosty who chooses gifts drawn from nature to reflect his gratitude.

> A joyful celebration of imagination, nature, and intergenerational storytelling that will warm hearts across snowy seasons and sunny days alike.

What inspired you to transition from teaching and farming to writing children's literature, and how has this journey been so far?

A tragic loss left me the single mom of 3 teens, a full time teacher and sole farm owner for many challenging years. When my eldest took over the farm, I moved to the lake, saw my daughters through university, remarried, looked after my parents and travelled a bit. I had been writing editorials, poetry, life stories and journals all along but retirement finally gave me the time to write. With my family cheering me on, notepads full of scribbles transformed into stories and now my dreams are my reality. The journey remains joyful and "Epp-ic"!

Can you elaborate on the significance of nature in your writing, especially considering your residence near Lake Erie and a National Park?

Living on the farm, by the lake and near Point Pelee, a world famous path of migratory birds, has been amazing. The jays, cardinals and Canada Geese just had to appear in my story. Hawk, Fox and Hare who reside here couldn't be left out! Every story I compose tends to highlight the flora and fauna of the natural world around me. The very bossy backyard bluejay is quite likely my next character!

How do you incorporate your role as a grandmother into your storytelling, and how does it resonate with young readers?

I show students my granddaughter's picture and explain how we co-created Ice Cap complete with cool glasses, a snowboard and an ice blue hat that charges his cell phone. Children are excited when they know a 4 sentence story from a 4 year old inspired my book. Many ask if they could write a book and I always say, "YES!" As a "safety-first" kind of gramma, I discuss technology. Kids agree a mobile phone is a fine tool but playing outside is way more fun than being glued to a screen all day. They think I'm a pretty cool gramma!

What challenges did you face while writing "Ice Cap," and how did you overcome them to bring the story to life?

Expediency was a big concern. I told Audrey I'd get Ice Cap published and had to promptly keep my promise. I spent months spinning a tale with poetic precision. I researched and contracted the hybrid publisher I trusted. Expenses were eye-opening but owning the rights to a legacy was worth every little job I took on to fund it. The BiblioKids' editors were pros and I was part of the process. The illustrator, Claire Sedovic, honoured my sketch of Ice Cap and her artistry made every page magical. But the moment Audrey held her own copy, "Ice Cap" came to life!

How do you engage with your audience, particularly children, during school visits and other events to promote "Ice Cap"?

Wherever I read "Ice Cap" I often pause to get students to reflect or have them chime in as we read. Little ones take turns holding my stuffed animals for a cozy experience. All ages are intrigued by the real items from my book like maple sugar sticks, thistle down, and jay feathers, etc. that I bring along to explore. Photos of B.C.'s well known boarder, Thomas Whittaker, actually holding my book is shown to every audience as he embodies Ice Cap's cool brand of kindness. Audiences love the real-life connection to my story. I've donated books to schools, libraries, toy drives and even hospitals to promote it but also to give back to the community. Each book I sell personally or at an event comes with a small toy. Local newspapers, local stores, podcasters, school websites and even Santa have been very helpful in promoting my work.

> *Ice Cap* by Joan Epp follows a magical snowman who brings joy, kindness, and fun during the winter months. With playful rhymes and whimsical illustrations, this story spreads messages of friendship, generosity, and winter magic. Ideal for children aged 3-7, it's a heartwarming, seasonal favourite for all ages.

What advice would you offer to aspiring authors looking to create engaging and educational children's books?

First, read to the age group you're writing for and find out which stories hold their attention. Seek the most popular books in your genre as they may possess the elements, style, or relevant themes that could make your story stand out. Write your story with authenticity, make sure it flows and read it aloud to children. Get professional critiques and polish your gem so it sparkles with imagination!

Exploring Themes Of Resilience, Morality, And Complex Characters

Joe Clark discusses how his diverse experiences influence his writing, exploring personal challenges and societal themes through richly developed characters in his novels.

JOE CLARK

UNVEILS HIS JOURNEY FROM ENGINEER TO AWARD-WINNING AUTHOR

By Z. Roberts I London

"Military service was a rude awakening for me."

Joe Clark's journey from a disciplined upbringing in Norfolk, Virginia, to the creative landscapes of literature is nothing short of remarkable. His incisive storytelling draws upon a wealth of experience—both personal and professional—that shapes the vivid narratives found in his novels. Award-winning and acclaimed, Clark's works invite readers to explore the intricate interplay between personal challenges and societal issues, deftly weaving themes of resilience, morality, and the complexities of human nature.

Clark's debut novel, *Survive*, introduces readers to Captain Lisa Maxwell, whose struggles to adapt after her service in Afghanistan resonate deeply in an era where the impacts of military life are increasingly scrutinised. Following this, *The Walshes* plunges into the enigmatic world of April Walsh, a suburban housewife who bravely navigates the murky waters of the sex industry. This bold exploration of taboo subjects showcases Clark's commitment to unflinching honesty in his character portrayals.

Recognised for his exceptional writing, Clark's novel *Demented* received long-list recognition for the Book Viral Millennium Book Award, affirming his status as a formidable voice in contemporary fiction. With each story, he crafts "deliciously flawed" characters who reflect real-world dilemmas, making his narratives not just relatable, but also profoundly impactful.

As readers engage with Clark's work, they are invited to traverse the landscapes of his life—through the trials of military service, the rigours of a technical career, and the poignant reflections on loss and resilience. This interview offers a glimpse into the mind of an author whose dedication to storytelling serves as an inspiration for aspiring writers and a delight for literature enthusiasts alike.

How did your experiences serving in Vietnam and your subsequent career in telecommunications influence the themes and characters in yournovels?

Military service was a rude awakening for me. I had been raised in a strict Catholic family and attended Catholic schools. I even spent some time studying for the priesthood.

Army life was the exact opposite of that upbringing. It was crude and amoral. I was forced to become comfortable with a seamier lifestyle. April Walsh faces a similar awakening in The Walshes when she takes on an assignment to write an expose of the sex industry.

My career as a telecommunications engineer coincides with my life as a married man. I married my first wife just before graduating from college and starting my career with Western Electric. Engineers and marriage figure prominently in my stories.

April's husband, Joe, is an engineer looking for a job after having been laid off, a situation I have dealt with several times. In Demented, Cindy's husband, Eric, is a computer systems engineer.

Mac in MacGregor's Final Battle is a retired engineer who had recently lost his wife of 40 years.

> Joe Clark is a masterful storyteller whose poignant narratives and complex characters captivate readers and inspire aspiring writers to pursue their craft.

In *"Survive,"* Army Captain Lisa Maxwell faces significant personal and external challenges upon returning from Afghanistan. What inspired you to create her character and her journey?

Lisa Maxwell was inspired by then Congresswoman, now Senator Tammy Duckworth, who was injured when her helicopter was shot down in Iraq.

***"The Walshes"* delves into the life of April Walsh, a suburban housewife who embarks on an undercover investigation into sex work. What motivated you to explore such a complex and controversial topic?**

While writing "Survive", I discovered writing sex scenes is challenging. Like many other writers, I was squeamish about putting the details in print.

I decided to write a story in which my female main character would be routinely in situations that required detailed descriptions of sex. But I didn't want her to be a prostitute with or without a heart of gold. April Walsh, suburban housewife and aspiring writer, takes on an undercover investigation of the sex industry in nearby Washington, D.C. and ends up working as an escort. She is an outsider learning about the business as she digs up information for her story.

Your novel *"Demented"* was long-listed for the Book Viral Millennium Book Award in 2020. How did this recognition impact your writing career?

The recognition means a lot to me. It shows an appreciation of my work by people who have never met me. That is a real boost to my confidence. It helps me continue writing.

It has not helped me find an agent or a publisher. I have not seen any evidence that it has boosted book sales.

After a 40-year career in telecommunications, what prompted you to pursue writing full-time, and how has your technical background influenced your storytelling?

This is a return to writing for me. I have been a writer all my life and a successful one in small venues. In 1984, I began working toward getting my stuff published. In January 1985, my wife died. Family responsibilities and a demanding job forced me to put my writing career on hold.

After I retired, I had time. I got involved with some writers' groups. One encouraged me to write Survive, my first novel. Another helped me figure out how to publish it.

I steer away from deep dives into technology – I don't think they belong in novels. My science and engineering did come into play in Survive when my characters got into working with radioactive materials. I had to keep reminding myself that the terrorists were building the bombs, not me.

I want readers to see and experience life through my characters.

Your characters often face moral and ethical dilemmas in challenging situations. How do you approach developing these "deliciously flawed" characters?

I seem to have a knack for developing relatable characters. I give them flaws that are exposed by the situations they find themselves in.

April Walsh has committed to the standard moral code for married women, but she is ambitious. Faced with a choice between violating that code or doing nothing, she ditches the code.

Bridget Allen was a normal, strong intelligent woman who loved her kids and her parents but married a weak, abusive man. After ending the marriage she discovered that sex work pays better than office work.

Adan Jackson is sadistic and rich. He gets his way too easily. He has no sense of limits.

Jack Edwards is guided by his sense of right and wrong more than by the law. When he meets Eve, he realizes what she's doing is illegal, but he sees her as a good person. He believes Troy Mondale was railroaded, so he's reluctant to pursue evidence that Troy committed a crime when he met with the Jacksons.

> *MacGregor's Final Battle* by Joe Clark" tells the poignant story of Donald MacGregor, who, facing terminal cancer, embarks on a journey in an RV. Along the way, he meets nurse Kate Graham, and together they explore their fears and hopes, forging a deep connection that transforms their lives amidst life's uncertainties.

Having traveled to your ancestral homes in Scotland and Ireland, have these experiences influenced any settings or themes in your books?

The travels have not influenced my writing so far.

What advice would you offer to aspiring authors who are transitioning from a different career into writing?

Be sure you're in it for the long haul. Instant successes are rare. Hope for the best, but prepare for the worst.

Study the craft. Read some of the excellent books available. The Great Courses by The Teaching Company include some excellent videos that aren't outrageously expensive.

Work with other writers – help them and get their help.

Exploring the Depths of Character and Consequence

Joe Kilgore shares insights into his writing process, the influence of advertising on storytelling, and crafting compelling characters. He discusses suspense, moral dilemmas, and offers advice for aspiring fiction writers.

JOE KILGORE
WEAVES SUSPENSE AND MASTERFUL STORYTELLING INTO UNFORGETTABLE FICTION

By Dan Peters I London

"My technique for maintaining the attention of the reader is to borrow the use of brevity that advertising requires."

Joe Kilgore is a name synonymous with gripping narratives, sharp storytelling, and an undeniable mastery of suspense. An award-winning writer of novels, novellas, screenplays, and short stories, Kilgore has carved an impressive literary path, blending his extensive background in advertising with his innate ability to craft unforgettable characters and unpredictable twists. His most recent novel, *Twelve Palominos*, a crime-mystery that showcases his signature tension-building and masterful pacing, is a testament to his talent for drawing readers into vividly realised worlds where every decision carries weight and consequence.

From the psychological complexity of his characters to the moral dilemmas that underpin his stories, Kilgore's works resonate with those who appreciate depth, nuance, and a touch of the unexpected. His short story collection, *Insomniac*, explores themes of karma and fate with a compelling intensity, while his critically acclaimed *Carrion Moon* has left readers stunned with its shocking revelations. Beyond his own writing, Kilgore's keen eye for storytelling extends to his work as a professional novel reviewer, offering insightful critiques that reflect his deep understanding of the craft.

In this exclusive *Reader's House* interview, Kilgore opens up about the intricacies of his writing process, the influence of his advertising career on his narrative style, and the art of keeping readers on the edge of their seats. His thoughts on character development, storytelling transitions between screen and page, and the delicate balance between structure and spontaneity provide invaluable insights for aspiring authors and seasoned writers alike.

A literary force who understands both the mechanics and magic of fiction, Joe Kilgore continues to captivate audiences with every story he tells. It is with great pleasure that we present this conversation with a writer who truly knows how to keep the pages turning.

How has your extensive background in advertising influenced the pacing and structure of your novels, particularly in creating suspenseful narratives?

Writing advertising requires precise discipline in space and time. Often you have only thirty seconds or less to make someone aware of what you are selling as well as providing the attributes of your product or service persuasively. Writing novels gives you the luxury of more space but is even more dependent upon holding reader interest. My technique for maintaining the attention of the reader is to borrow the use of brevity that advertising requires, while simultaneously sticking to prose, plot, and character arcs that always move the story forward. As famous novelist and screenwriter Elmore Leonard once advised, simply "take out the parts that readers will skip over anyway."

Joe Kilgore masterfully blends suspense, character depth, and sharp storytelling, creating gripping narratives that captivate, surprise, and leave readers enthralled.

In your short story collection, "Insomniac," you explore themes of karma and consequences. How do you decide which themes to delve into?

I follow the maxim, write what you like to read. I've always been drawn to literature and film that highlights individuals' capacity to function under pressure. Often, I try to develop situations and scenarios that give a protagonist multiple ways to deal with trouble. Some good ways, some bad. Then I'll frequently have he or she make an even worse decision than was made before, escalating the degree of angst. Reading about terrible things in other peoples' lives makes folks even more sanguine that they are in their shoes and not the characters.

Your novels often feature complex characters facing moral dilemmas. What draws you to these characters, and how do you develop them?

Complex people are simply more interesting than dullards. As a reader, I'd rather spend time with a highly accomplished sociopath than an everyday pensioner. Unless of course, that pensioner happens to be a closet serial killer. People with lives particularly unlike my own are the ones I find most interesting. So I often go out of my way to create characters that feel real, but are laden with poor judgement, quirks, and peccadillos that constantly intrude on their ability to avoid misfortune. I enjoy creating men and women who are active participants in their own demise.

Given your experience writing screenplays, how do you adapt your storytelling techniques when transitioning from screen to page?

One can be more expansive on the page than on the screen. You can dive deeper into what one is thinking rather than simply what one is doing. You don't have to worry about the increased time and additional cost of a relevant flashback or a Daliesque dream sequence. But one should still keep the techniques that add to involvement. When appropriate, show rather than say, dramatize rather than describe, choose illustration over exposition. Rely on a book reader's imagination. It's frequently more involved than a movie goer's.

Carrion Moon has been praised for its shocking twists. How do you craft these twists to maintain reader engagement and surprise?

Think of what the initial answer to a question would be and provide a different one. Consider how a logical progression would be used to solve a problem and provide a perhaps less logical but more interesting evolution. When the villain is to be unmasked, make sure it's not the one most readers would assume it to be. Don't forsake credibility for shock or surprise, but don't let the reader know exactly where you're going until you get there. Always come up with a compelling reason for him or her to turn the page.

As a professional novel reviewer, how do you balance critical analysis with your creative writing, and does one influence the other?

A review should be written as interestingly as the novel it's reviewing. The more stylish the review, the more interested one will be to pick up or pass by the tome. When engaged in reviewing, discuss content, plot, characterization, etc., by elucidating what is done well or ill by dissecting the author's words rather than his or her intent. When writing creatively, paint the word picture you want to show, but leave it to the reader to supply his or her own interpretation. In my particular case, I believe my reviews are influenced more by my creative writing than the other way round.

San Diego PI Brig Ellis is hired to secure the last of twelve palomino miniatures linked to China's last emperor. What starts as a simple job turns perilous, involving criminals, kidnappers, and a ruthless assassin. With danger escalating, Ellis must navigate deadly obstacles to survive and complete his mission.

What advice would you offer to aspiring authors aiming to transition from a successful career in advertising to writing fiction?

For most, the answer can be found in the wise counsel of he who first said, "Don't quit your day job." If you can do both, do both. Advertising often proceeds at warp speed. Writing fiction is more akin to glacial melting. Not necessarily in the writing itself, but in the submitting, the acceptance or rejection, the frequently enormous amount of time that transpires between the time you finish writing something and someone tells you he's willing to publish it. Writing advertising is almost always more lucrative as well. But if you have stories in you that simply must be told, write them. Then to borrow a phrase, stick your perseverance to the sticking place. You'll need all of it you can muster. Of course, as many assume, if you have only one life to live, and you feel that you must live it as a writer, by all means, do so.

Rethinking Earth's History Through Science, Myth And Catastrophe

Joseph O'Donoghue challenges conventional geology with a bold theory linking Ice Age catastrophes to the legend of Atlantis, grounded in evidence and the laws of physics.

JOSEPH O'DONOGHUE

UNCOVERS THE GEOLOGICAL SECRETS BEHIND THE ATLANTIS LEGEND

By Ben Alan I London

Joseph O'Donoghue brings a rare combination of scientific training and independent inquiry to the enduring mysteries of our planet's past. With a background in geology and decades of personal research, he has ventured beyond conventional academic boundaries to re-examine some of the most puzzling geological phenomena — particularly those surrounding the Ice Age and the lost civilisation of Atlantis. His work challenges mainstream doctrines with a rigorous, physics-based approach, drawing attention to overlooked evidence and encouraging a rethinking of Earth's catastrophic history.

In this interview, O'Donoghue shares the motivations behind his quest, his scepticism toward uniformitarian principles, and the compelling connections he believes link geology with ancient myth.

"The fact that the end of the Ice Age coincides with the end of Atlantis was intriguing and begged investigation."

What inspired you to explore the connection between geology and the Atlantis legend?

My initial inspiration derived from a certain skepticism I developed toward a number of theories and principles met with during my years at university. The fact that the end of the Ice Age coincides with the end of Atlantis was intriguing and begged investigation, and doubly so since a number of other major events are also seen to have occurred at the time in question. Further, if a continent sank in the North Atlantic, then it must have done so by some geological process, of which evidence should still be there to be found.

How do you approach reconciling geological evidence with ancient myths like Atlantis?

I begin with a study of the evidence and a study of the legend, whatever it might be. The key to my approach is to ignore standard geological theory, which has no room for legends such as Atlantis. I bring an open mind to any question and my primary assessment of all geological evidence is through the lens of physics.

In your research, which geological discoveries have most significantly challenged orthodox geological theories?

Probably the most significant and well-known discovery is that of the multitudes of Pleistocene mammals such as mammoths, rhinoceros, auroch, horses, etc., etc., found frozen all across the arctic regions, especially in Siberia. Despite the denials of orthodox geology, these multitudes of frozen animals attest to a great catastrophe at the end of the Ice Age.

> A thought-provoking voice in geological science, offering fresh insight into ancient mysteries with clarity, courage, and a deeply analytical mind.

Can you elaborate on the role of catastrophism in your work and why it should be considered in modern geology?

It's not so much that catastrophism plays a role in my work, as in my approach to any evidence, so much as my work indicates that catastrophes have played a role in the geological history of this planet. In other words, I don't start with a bias, but with an open mind toward any body of evidence. As for catastrophism in modern geology, I certainly maintain that the possibility of major catastrophes in earth history is very real.

What are the most compelling pieces of evidence that support the existence of Atlantis, in your view?

The legend states that, at the same time that Atlantis sank beneath the waves, ancient Greece suffered a catastrophe involving major flooding over Greece. As I detail in my volume 2, the geological evidence attests to just such a catastrophe of widespread water action, and not to mention the worn-down condition of the Acropolis itself.

How do you think traditional geological theories, like uniformitarianism, have hindered the exploration of alternative explanations for Earth's history?

Uniformitarianism as a governing paradigm has the effect of constraining thinking to within the confines of a slow, gradual, and uneventful earth history, and, since all students are essentially indoctrinated at university, alternatives are not even considered.

What advice would you give to aspiring authors who wish to tackle controversial topics in science while maintaining a rigorous, evidence-based approach?

My primary advice would be to use an open-minded approach and focus on gathering all the evidence first, and ignore all standard theories of its formation. Secondarily, this evidence should then be tested against any laws of physics that pertain to that evidence.

The Legend of Atlantis and The Science of Geology by Joseph O'Donoghue examines the Atlantis legend through a scientific lens, challenging conventional geological theories. The book explores both geological and mythological perspectives, critically analysing Atlantis' validity and exploring global catastrophe myths, proposing that modern geology may not fully account for historical events.

A Journey from Grandmother to Award-Winning Author

Liliana Tommasini discusses her inspiration, challenges, and journey as a children's book author. She shares insights on diversity in storytelling, her role as an Author Coach, and advice for aspiring writers.

LILIANA TOMMASINI

INSPIRES YOUNG READERS THROUGH THE OCTAVIA CAN DO IT! SERIES

BY READER'S HOUSE STAFF

"That simple yet heartfelt gesture truly touched my heart—I still have that colouring sheet to this day."

Liliana Tommasini has a remarkable gift for weaving stories that not only entertain but also empower children to embrace curiosity, independence, and resilience. As the author of the *Octavia Can Do It!* series, she brings to life a spirited young girl who learns the balance between self-reliance and seeking support—an invaluable lesson for children navigating their own journeys.

Her passion for storytelling stems from a deeply personal place: her grandchildren. Struggling to find books that reflected their experiences, Liliana took matters into her own hands, crafting stories that celebrate diversity and encourage young readers to explore the world around them with confidence. With a keen understanding of what truly resonates with children, she has created books that spark joy, foster self-belief, and leave a lasting impression.

Beyond her work as an author, Liliana is also an Author Coach, guiding aspiring writers through the intricate process of bringing their own stories to life. Her journey—from hesitant beginnings to becoming a published author with a growing series—stands as an inspiration to those who dream of sharing their own tales with the world.

In this interview with *Reader's House magazine*, Liliana shares the heart-warming inspirations behind her books, the challenges she has overcome, and the wisdom she imparts to both young readers and aspiring authors alike.

What inspired you to write children's books, particularly the Octavia Can Do It! series?

I was inspired to write children's books when my grandchildren were born. I began reading to them at a young age as their parents did. Since my grandchildren are multi-ethnic, I struggled to find books with characters they could relate to—so I decided to write one myself.

How do you incorporate your grandchildren's experiences into your stories?.

As I watch them grow, I notice the unique qualities each of them possesses. Octavia is a spirited girl who enjoys being independent and believes she can handle things on her own without asking for help. In 'Octavia Can Do It!', she comes to realize that sometimes, it's okay to ask for assistance.

What challenges have you faced as a children's book author, and how have you overcome them?.

At first, I felt overwhelmed and unsure of where to begin or if I was even making the right choice—I never saw myself as an author. After extensive research, I decided to join a reputable hybrid publishing company that offered a children's writing course. They also provided in-house editors, book designers, mastermind meetings, and author coaches to guide me through the writing journey.

Liliana Tommasini crafts heartfelt stories that celebrate diversity, inspire confidence, and empower children to embrace curiosity, independence, and resilience.

Being part of this writing community gave me the confidence to write my first two books in the Octavia Can Do It! series, with the third book set to be published in 2025.

Can you share a memorable reaction or feedback from a child who read your books?

One of my most cherished moments was when my oldest daughter, Camelia, and I hosted a reading and colouring session at a day summer camp. At the end of the session, a little girl handed me her coloring sheet with her name on it, beaming with a big smile. That simple yet heartfelt gesture truly touched my heart—I still have that coloring sheet to this day.

What do you think is the most important lesson children can take away from your books?

As I watched my grandchildren grow, I

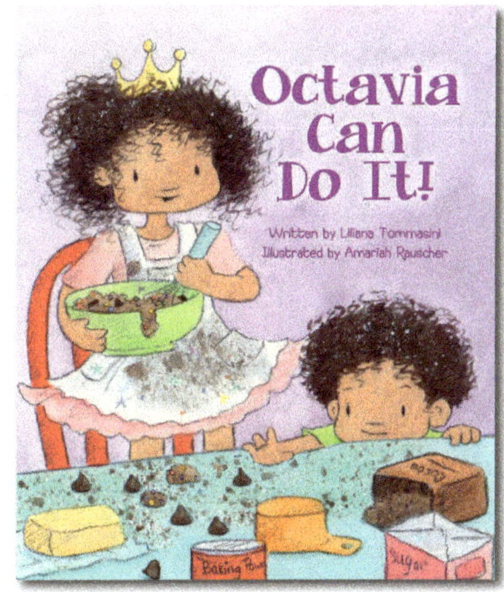

Octavia loves baking with her Mama, but today she wants to do it all by herself. As flour and cocoa cover the kitchen, she begins to doubt her skills. *Octavia Can Do It!* is a humorous, heartwarming story about independence, learning from mistakes, and realising that everyone needs help sometimes.

encouraged them to explore, discover new things on their own, and ask for help when needed. This is the message I hope to share with children through my stories.

How does your role as an Author Coach influence your own writing process?

As an Author Coach, I help aspiring children's book authors bring their stories to life. Guiding them through their writing journey is not just about teaching. It's a two-way street that helps me improve my own writing of what stories connect with children and leave a lasting impact.

What advice would you give to aspiring children's book authors looking to publish their first book?

Every writer faces challenges, no matter where they are in their journey. Those challenges can lead you to some amazing support. If you're feeling stuck with your story, consider joining a writing group on social media or signing up for a class. It can really help to connect with others who get it. Also, look at different types of publishing companies and see what they offer to help you share your story. And most importantly, keep going! Above all, don't give up on writing - you have your own unique story to tell!

A Journey Into The Essence Of Love And Existence

Raz Mihal's work unveils divine love as an eternal force, offering readers a deeper understanding of love beyond human definitions.

RAZ MIHAL

EXPLORES DIVINE LOVE IN HIS PROFOUND NEW WORK

Editor's Desk I London

Raz Mihal is a writer, philosopher, and spiritual seeker whose work explores the boundless nature of divine love. His book *Just Love Her* is not merely an exploration of romantic love but an invitation to experience love as an eternal, living force that transcends societal norms and personal expectations. With a background in spirituality, meditation, and philosophical inquiry, Raz's writing emerges from direct experience, offering readers a deeper understanding of love as the very essence of existence.

In this exclusive interview for *Reader's House Magazine*, Raz discusses the profound moments that shaped his spiritual journey, the role of love in our daily lives, and how his insights continue to evolve.

"That night was a profound awakening that forever changed my perception of love, reality, and existence itself."

What inspired you to explore the concept of divine love in your work?

My journey into divine love was not a decision but an unfolding—something that revealed itself over time rather than something I actively sought. It began as a deep, unshakable feeling, an awareness that love was far more than an emotion since childhood. Over the years, I understood love as the essence of existence through meditation, solitude, and reflection. This realisation was too profound to keep within—it needed to be shared. Writing became my bridge between the silence of contemplation and the voice that could express even a glimpse of this truth. Just Love Her was born from that space, not as a structured teaching but as an invitation for readers to experience love beyond the boundaries of thought, beyond what society defines as love, and to recognise it as the divine force that has always been within them.

How do you believe love transcends societal norms, and what impact does that have on our daily lives?

Love, in its purest form, exists beyond societal definitions, expectations, and conditions. Societal norms often treat love as transactional—something given and received based on circumstances, validation, or personal gain. But divine love is not dependent on action or reciprocation; it is an eternal state of being, the very fabric of existence. When we shift from viewing love as something to be earned or controlled to something that simply is, it transforms every aspect of our lives. Relationships become more authentic, free from fear and need. Compassion flows effortlessly because it is no longer bound by self-interest. The more we recognise that love is not something external but an ever-present force within, the more we allow it to shape our interactions, breaking down the illusion of separation between us and the world.

Can you explain the significance of the night of June 3rd to 4th, 1998, in shaping your spiritual journey and writing?

That night was a profound awakening that forever changed my perception of love, reality, and existence itself. It was not just an experience but an undeniable recognition of oneness with divine love, seeing it in everything that existed. For the first time, I realised that divine love was not a distant ideal or an abstract concept but a living energy present in all things—from life itself to the solidity of objects woven into the very fabric of existence. Everywhere I looked, I saw this raw essence of divine love, an unbreakable connection that transcended form and time.

> A spiritual journey that invites readers to awaken to the infinite presence of love in all things.

This revelation also transformed my understanding of solitude. Until that moment, I believed withdrawing from the world was necessary to seek truth, but that night, I understood that divine love is not separate from the world—it is the world. The beauty of existence is not in retreating from it but in living fully within it, embracing every moment as an expression of love itself.

Many years later, when I wrote Just Love Her, the essence of that night remained—unchanged yet always new, continuously unfolding, revealing different facets of the same eternal truth. That moment was not something I held onto as a memory but something I lived through every time I allowed love to flow through my words.

In your book Just Love Her, how does the setting of Seoul play a role in conveying the themes of human love and divine connection?

Seoul became more than just a backdrop—it was an extension of the journey itself, a place that felt familiar and unknown, as if my soul had already walked its streets long before I arrived. I had dreamt of this city months before, and even years later, the connection remained—an unspoken resonance that felt like remnants of a past imprinted on my soul.

Walking through Seoul, I was surrounded by contrasts—modernity and tradition, solitude and movement, longing and presence. Yet, beyond these contrasts, I sensed a deeper reality unfolding. The city's history, struggles, and the silent echoes of suffering opened the door to my heart, revealing love in ways I had not anticipated. It was not just a love for a place but a revelation through love itself—love that transcended time and connected souls beyond physical existence.

Through this lens, I understood that my soul was intertwined with another—a connection to a Korean girl who, simultaneously, was both herself and the divine love incarnate through the presence of divine love inside. She was not just a person but a living reflection of love's infinite essence, an embodiment of the truth that divine love manifests in the world, taking form while remaining boundless. This recognition was not about attachment but awakening—an unveiling of love as the ultimate reality, interwoven through all things.

Seoul's setting reinforced this truth: love is not bound by space or circumstance. It is something we awaken to, something that has always existed within us, waiting to be remembered.

What do you envision as the future of love, particularly in a world influenced by technology and artificial intelligence?

Technology and artificial intelligence are reshaping how we connect, but the essence of love remains unchanged. The challenge is that as our digital world expands, there is a risk of love being further reduced to convenience, validation, or algorithmic compatibility—stripped of its depth, spontaneity, and mystery. However, true love, especially divine love, cannot be replicated or replaced. No matter how advanced AI becomes, it cannot generate the depth of awareness that arises from a soul recognising itself in another.

Yet, technology also has the potential to serve love rather than diminish it. If used consciously, it can create bridges, connect souls across distances, and facilitate greater understanding. The future of love depends on whether we allow technology to shape our perception of love or if we use technology as a tool while remaining rooted in love as a state of being—one that cannot be programmed or predicted but only felt and lived.

How do you personally define enlightenment, and how does it relate to your perspective on love?

Enlightenment is not an end goal but an awakening to what has always been. It is the recognition that love is not something separate from us, not something to be chased or acquired, but something that has existed within us since the beginning. It is the moment we stop searching and start being, allowing love to flow through us without condition, without attachment.

Many seek enlightenment as if it were an achievement, but it is simply remembering what was never lost. Love and enlightenment are inseparable because to awaken genuinely is to realise that love is the essence of existence itself. The more we open ourselves to love—not as emotion, not as attachment, but as the divine force that binds all things—the closer we come to understanding who we are.

> *Just Love Her* by Raz Mihal is a poetic and spiritual exploration of divine love and soul connection. Through meditative reflections, Mihal presents love as a transformative, guiding force, encouraging readers to embrace the divine feminine and experience love beyond time and form. A heartfelt guide for spiritual growth and self-discovery.

What advice would you give to other authors who are interested in writing about profound spiritual or philosophical concepts?

Write from experience, not from theory. Spirituality and philosophy are not ideas to be studied—they are truths to be lived. If the words do not come from a place of direct experience, they will remain concepts rather than insights that truly reach the reader.

Also, do not be afraid of abstraction. Some truths cannot be explained in direct language; that is where metaphor, poetry, and allegory become potent tools. At the same time, remember the reader—invite them into the experience rather than just presenting an idea. Let them feel the journey rather than just read about it.

Most importantly, trust the process. Profound writing cannot be forced. It emerges when the writer allows themselves to be fully present in the experience, letting the words flow naturally, without the need to control or perfect them. Just as love cannot be grasped but only recognised, authentic writing happens when you stop trying to write and allow the truth to express itself.

Romance and mystery just came out of my keyboard."

Celebrating A Life of Adventure, Creativity, and Storytelling

Tina Sloan shares how her acting career, adventurous spirit, and global travels shape her award-winning novels filled with romance, intrigue, and vibrant characters.

TINA SLOAN

INSPIRES READERS WITH HER THRILLING STORIES, LIFE LESSONS AND UNSTOPPABLE SPIRIT

as told to D. Peters

Tina Sloan is nothing short of a force of nature. A highly accomplished actress with a storied career spanning theatre, television, and film, she captivated audiences for decades with her portrayal of Lillian Raines on *Guiding Light*, one of television's most beloved soap operas. Beyond the screen, however, Tina has dazzled the literary world with her transition from actress to author, proving that her talent knows no bounds. Her books are a testament to her ability to weave drama, romance, and intrigue into evocative page-turners that transport readers across the globe.

From her heartfelt debut *Changing Shoes*, which inspired a hugely successful one-woman show, to her award-winning *Chasing Cleopatra*, *Chasing Othello*, and the thrilling recent addition, *Chasing Czars*, Tina's writing is the result of a vivid imagination shaped by rich life experiences. An avid globetrotter, marathoner, and mountaineer, Tina brings her adventurous spirit to her characters, crafting resilient heroines and high-stakes narratives set against a backdrop of exotic locations. Whether immersing her readers in romance, espionage, or powerful reflections on life's transitions, her work bursts with authenticity, wit, and depth.

In this issue of *Reader's House*, Tina Sloan reflects on her journey from soap opera icon to bestselling author, her inspirations, and the art of reinvention. A woman who has conquered 20,000-foot peaks, both literally and metaphorically, her insights on writing and living with purpose are as compelling as the stories she tells. It's a pleasure to offer you this intimate conversation with an author who continues to inspire us on and off the page.

How did your experiences as an actress, particularly on The Guiding Light, influence your approach to writing novels?

Spending 30 years reading my 72-page scripts daily, 52 weeks a year, I was inundated by drama and secrets, love and jealousy, murder, romance, and surprise endings. These things leaked into my writing by osmosis. What I added was a great deal of research, but the plots just flowed from all those years on Guiding Light.

Chasing Cleopatra and Chasing Othello blend romance, espionage, and highstakes drama- what draws you to this mix of genres?

As a child, I loved Nancy Drew, and as a young adult, it was Agatha Christie. As an adult, books about spies like Kim Philby fascinated me. I always loved solving mysteries and still do, and I have thrived on romance my whole life, so as I wrote, romance and mystery just came out of my keyboard. .

Your book Chasing Shoes encourages women to embrace life's changes with style and humor- how has this philosophy shaped your own personal and professional journey?

CHANGING SHOES I wrote this book initially to help women deal with aging and with the family drama of aging parents and all the things the ends of life show us. It was easy for me to feel sorry for myself as I helped my parents into their 90s, so I decided to help others and, in turn, made it a discovery for myself. I wrote a one-woman show from the book, which was also called Changing Shoes. I did the show all over the US and in London. President and Barbara Bush came to see it in Houston, Texas!!

Tina Sloan is a powerhouse of creativity, blending her unmatched career experiences with heartfelt storytelling and an indomitable zest for life.

Cleopatra Gallier is a fascinating character- how much of her is inspired by your own life and adventures? You've climbed 20,000-foot peaks and run multiple marathons- do these achievements play a role in shaping your characters' resilience and determination?

Cleopatra is someone I would have had adventures with. I ran marathons in Honolulu as she did, I climbed Kilimanjaro in Africa, and I skied in St Moritz as she does. I had one child late in life, as she does, though she has a second child in CHASING CZARS, book 3 of the series, which just came out. In many ways, she is an alter ego, though I give her far more drama in her life than I have in mine. But having done strenuous things, I certainly wanted my heroine to have a zest for life and an attitude of making things seem easy.

What was the biggest challenge in transitioning from acting to writing, and what surprised you most about the process?

Transitioning from actress to author was FUN. I now had as much power over my characters' lives and deaths as the writers of Guiding Light had over me for decades.

Your books take readers from Hawaii to Dubai and beyond- how important is setting in your storytelling, and do you draw from your own travels?

My locations are another character in my novels. Dubai, Honolulu, and St Moritz are places I know well, having often spent vacations there. I love them as much as I love Cleo.

What advice would you offer to other authors, particularly those looking to transition from a different career into writing?

Put everything else aside. Be like Virginia Wolfe and have a room of your own, even if it is a closet. I think you need to have your partner stay away while you work. You must never get distracted by your iPhone or seeing friends for lunch. You need to be all in. Then, when the thoughts and the words start coming, you are ready, but sometimes they don't come, and that is all part of the game. I am not a plotter of a book. I just get surprised by what my characters choose to do. Many authors love to have it all laid out ahead. There are so many ways, but as Nike says, JUST DO IT!

Chasing Czars by Tamara Lush is a gripping spy thriller with an intelligent, endearing lead. The novel skilfully balances romance, history, and intrigue in a vivid, fast-paced narrative. Though some moments feel underexplored, it remains an engaging and stylish debut, perfect for fans of adventure, espionage, and strong, multifaceted heroines.

Empowering Children Through Words and Wisdom

Award-winning author Shani T. Night shares her passion for storytelling, the inspiration behind her books, and how positivity, self-expression, and personal growth shape both her writing and coaching.

SHANI T. NIGHT

INSPIRES YOUNG READERS AND TRANSFORMS LIVES THROUGH THE POWER OF STORYTELLING

"The heart of Shani and Friends revolves around learning, imagination, and the special moments of childhood."

Editot's Desk I London

Shani T. Night is a name synonymous with inspiration, empowerment, and heartfelt storytelling. As an award-winning children's author and Certified Happiness, Life, and Wellness Coach, she has dedicated her life to fostering joy, self-expression, and personal growth—both on the page and beyond. Her books are more than just stories; they are a guiding light for young readers, offering them the reassurance that they are seen, valued, and capable of overcoming life's challenges.

With a literary career spanning over four decades, Shani has woven magic into her words, crafting narratives that encourage self-discovery and resilience. Her beloved Shani and Friends series captures the wonder of childhood, celebrating friendship, curiosity, and the joy of learning. Meanwhile, her guided journals, including Intentionally Positive, provide tools for self-reflection and emotional growth, reflecting her deep understanding of the power of positivity. And with her upcoming release, The Whispers of Destiny: Guided by the Spirit Within, she once again proves that storytelling is not just about entertainment—it's about transformation.

In this exclusive interview with Reader's House, Shani shares her journey, the inspiration behind her works, and the profound impact of positive self-talk. Her words remind us that literature has the power to shape lives, and that through stories, we can teach the next generation to embrace their inner strength and shine their brightest.

What inspired you to begin writing children's books, and how has your journey evolved over the past 40 years?

My biggest inspiration for writing children's books is to bring comfort and joy to kids, especially those with invisible disabilities, by creating stories where they feel seen. I want my books to uplift, inspire, and encourage all children, offering them a sense of belonging and empowerment, no matter the challenges they face.

Though I've always dreamed of writing children's books, that dream was put on hold—until everything aligned at the right time. My husband, an author and illustrator, became my illustrator, helping bring my vision to life. My daughter, with her Digital Media degree, further shaped my books visually and conceptually. With the support of my family, my journey has evolved from a long-held dream to a meaningful reality, allowing me to create stories that inspire, uplift, and resonate with children everywhere.

Could you share the central themes and messages in your 'Shani and Friends' series?

Shani and Friends is a heartwarming series inspired by my childhood adventures, following six-year-old Shani as she discovers the joy of learning at school with friends and the wonder of exploring her home and garden. Each story is filled with excitement, curiosity, and everyday magic, celebrating the beauty of friendship, discovery, and the simple joys of childhood.

The heart of the series revolves around learning, imagination, and the special moments of childhood. The series was inspired by my childhood experiences that sparked my curiosity and contributed to my educational growth. Themes of friendship, family, self-discovery, kindness, and a passion for learning are all the themes I wanted to express in this series. Shani's adventures are designed to motivate children to maintain their sense of wonder and cherish their friends while experiencing happiness in everyday moments.

> Shani T. Night is a gifted storyteller whose heartfelt books inspire confidence, joy, and self-discovery in young readers worldwide.

How do you balance your roles as an author and a Certified Happiness, Life, and Wellness Coach in your storytelling?

Believe it or not, one wouldn't exist without the other. They are deeply connected. My love of writing directly shaped my storytelling, while my passion for helping through writing deeply influenced my coaching and helped me create books that inspire personal growth, positivity, and self-discovery. At the same time, through my books I communicate with people worldwide extending past individual coaching sessions, providing tools and messages that uplift readers looking for encouragement at their own pace. It's an infinite loop, each fueling the other. Whether coaching or storytelling, my mission remains the same: to inspire, uplift, and help others live their happiest, most fulfilling lives.

What motivated you to create the 'Intentionally Positive' guided journals, and how do they complement your books?

I was motivated by change. Guided journaling reshaped my life at a time when I needed it most. It softened how I respond to struggles, deepened how I see the world, and strengthened how I hold space for others. Through introspection, I gained clarity. With each reflection, I learned to stand in the fullness of my truth. And when you come to understand the true gift of journaling, there is only one thing left to do—share it.

Because I believe in the power of foundational work and my publisher embraces the Happy In, Happy Out philosophy, Intentionally Positive has become the heart of everything I create. It's not just the foundation for my self-help books but also for my children's books—because when positivity is nurtured early, it shapes how we grow, learn, and thrive.

How do you envision your upcoming book, 'The Whispers of Destiny: Guided by the Spirit Within,' impacting young readers?

I want The Whispers of Destiny to reach deep, to stir something inside young readers that does not fade. I want its impact to be more than words on a page—I want it to be a turning point, a light that lingers long after the final chapter. The lessons within are placed with care, because I have come to know a great truth: we are far more alike than we imagine.

If children are given the gift of introspection, if they learn early the power of looking within, then what greater offering is there? What better way to extend a hand, to ease the weight for the ones who come after us? It is like smoothing the path just enough, so they do not stumble where we once did. If they walk away knowing, truly knowing, that they are enough, then the work, the words, the journey, will have been worth it. Emma's journey and the lessons she learns are designed to reflect these very truths, guiding young readers toward self-discovery and resilience.

Can you discuss the significance of positive self-talk in your work, particularly in 'Positive Self-Talk: Transforming Your Silent Thoughts'?

Life-changing. There are books that entertain, books that inform, and then there are books that change you. Positive Self-Talk is one of those books. You don't always know what you need until you find it and this book changes your mindset. The beauty of this book is that it provides real-life examples and exercises that help readers reshape their inner dialogue.

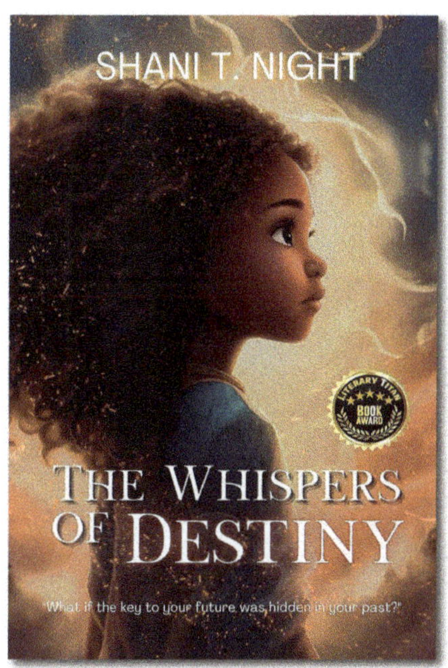

> Twelve-year-old Emma embarks on a time-travel journey guided by a mysterious spirit, tasked with unlocking her inner strength to shape a brighter future. As she uncovers family secrets and deepens her bond with her mother, Emma must navigate destiny, free will, and the fragile balance of time itself.

I know the power of self-talk because I have lived it. I have seen how words—whether lifted in love or weighed down in doubt—shape the world around me. Each time I spoke negativity into existence, it answered. But when I chose a different language, a kinder, truer one, life answered in kind. Because words are not just words. They are the seeds of who we become.

How do you incorporate your personal experiences and values into your stories to inspire young readers?

Every book I've written begins with truth—a real story and a spark of inspiration. I've found that I can only write from a place of authenticity. While imagination plays a role, it's the truth woven into the story that gives it depth and meaning. Without that, the words wouldn't carry the same impact or joy.

What advice would you offer to aspiring authors aiming to write children's books that inspire and empower young minds?

Just go for it! Start with a message that truly speaks to your heart, and let that be your foundation. The passion and inspiration will follow—I know this from experience.

Stenetta Anthony Educator to Children's Author

Stenetta Anthony discusses her transition from teaching to writing, the themes in her books, and her passion for storytelling.

"The message I hope that young readers take away from this book is to remain positive, have confidence, and be persistent."

STENETTA ANTHONY

INSPIRES YOUNG MINDS WITH HER AWARD-WINNING CHILDREN'S BOOKS

Editor's Desk I London

Stenetta Anthony is a celebrated author whose passion for storytelling has taken her from the classroom to the world of children's literature. With over a decade of experience as an educator, Stenetta has a unique perspective on the challenges and triumphs children face, which she seamlessly weaves into her books. Her works, such as *Ella Learns to Dance* and *A Home for Sally*, highlight themes of inclusivity, empowerment, and resilience—values she has long championed in her teaching career.

In this interview with *Reader's House Magazine*, Stenetta shares her inspiring journey from educator to award-winning author, discussing how her background informs her writing and the importance of creating stories that resonate with young readers.

How did your 22-year tenure as an educator influence the themes and stories you choose to write about in your children's books?

My time in the classroom has taught me the importance of inclusiveness and has had a profound effect on my writing. It is important for me to feature diverse characters and settings that children from all backgrounds can relate to. I've seen first-hand how children often struggle with inadequacy, fear, loneliness, disappointment and rejection, just to name a few. These experiences and many others have had an influence on the themes and stories I choose when writing my children's books.

What inspired you to transition from teaching to writing, and how has your educational background shaped your approach to storytelling?

Storytelling is something I have enjoyed since childhood. As a child I often recreated books that I read into different characters and themes and retold them to my younger siblings. I have brought this love for storytelling to the classroom as part of my teaching style. Therefore, the transition from teaching to writing and my love for storytelling is a combination of my passion and creativity.

Could you share the inspiration behind your book "Ella Learns to Dance" and what message you hope young readers take away from it?

Dance is a powerful metaphor I choose to use for "Ella Learns to Dance." I wanted to dispel some challenges and misconceptions that are sometimes associated with a specific genre of dance. Focusing on what some children may experience on their way to accomplishing their dreams. The message I hope that young readers take away from this book is twofold, first it's okay that everyone does not approve of your dream and that you must remain positive, have confidence and be persistent so you can reach your goals.

Stenetta's work is widely celebrated for its meaningful messages, with her books praised for their powerful themes and diverse characters.

"A Home for Sally" addresses themes of belonging and acceptance. What motivated you to tackle this subject, and how have readers responded to the story?

The purpose for, "A Home for Sally comes from my experiences as an educator working with diverse learners.. The books that were available to them did not represent children like them. Many of these children (from my experience) face the struggle with being accepted as, "being beautiful and normal," by some children and adults. I have witnessed how some of my students and others reacted to their feelings of rejection. This topic is especially close to my heart because I believe that fostering a sense of belonging in all children from a young age builds a foundation for confidence and resilience. This book has been well received and considered, "A treasure of a book with a powerful message. "- Emily-Jane Hills Orford

Your book "31 Days of Treasure" offers daily insights. What was your goal in creating this collection, and how do you envision it being used by families and educators?

When writing 31 Days of Treasures, I envisioned it as a free resource, which can be used by individuals', educators and others to guide them through their daily life. We discuss a variety of topics and give valuable insight. Thus creating an open and honest dialogue for discussion. I envision 31 Days of Treasures being used to create curriculums, lesson plans and for group discussions for both the private and public sectors of education. With families also using this collection as a resource to instill their individual family values. Although these are some of the things I saw for this collection; however, my primary purpose for creating this collection is to be used in bringing positive changes into individual lives.

Having earned a degree in educational leadership in 2018, how has this advanced education impacted your writing and the themes you explore in your books?

My perspective has changed to focus not only on individual achievement. I am more attuned to what children face in diverse settings, so my characters and narratives are a reflection of the challenges and accomplishments experienced by readers. In my writing I have found myself exploring themes about empowerment, persistence and acceptance. This educational leadership degree has become a central part of my writing development.

You've received several accolades, including the Mom's Choice Award and recognition from Midwest Book Review. How have these honours influenced your career, and what do they mean to you personally?

For some authors, they are confident and proudly call themselves authors; however, this was not me. For many years I did not feel like an author. So, receiving the Mom's Choice Award along with others along with recognition from Midwest Book Reviews was sobering and humbling. Receiving these accolades-built self-confidence as an author, now I am proud to say I am an author, while advancing my career. Where I can now say I am not only an author but an award-winning author.

What advice would you offer to aspiring authors, especially those aiming to write impactful children's literature?

The advice I would give is to use the correct language and themes appropriate for their specific ages. Tell a meaningful story that resonates with children, such as friendship, resilience, acceptance and kindness. Create memorable and relatable characters, avoid stereotypes and keep your story engaging from beginning to end. Some authors only consider the writing process; however, you must also become familiar with the business of writing, publishing, finances, and contractual agreements. Build a platform for your literary works using various methods. Most of all, be confident and be patient with yourself.

Ella Learns to Dance is a heartwarming story about an elephant named Ella who dreams of becoming a ballet dancer. Despite discouragement from a friend, she remains determined. This inspiring tale encourages children to believe in themselves, follow their passions, and embrace their uniqueness, no matter the obstacles.

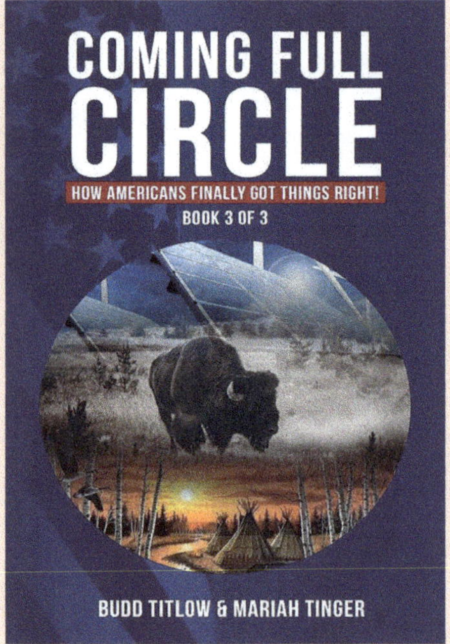

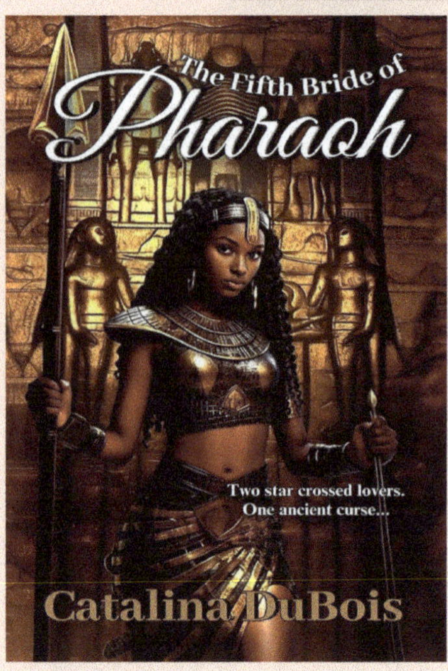

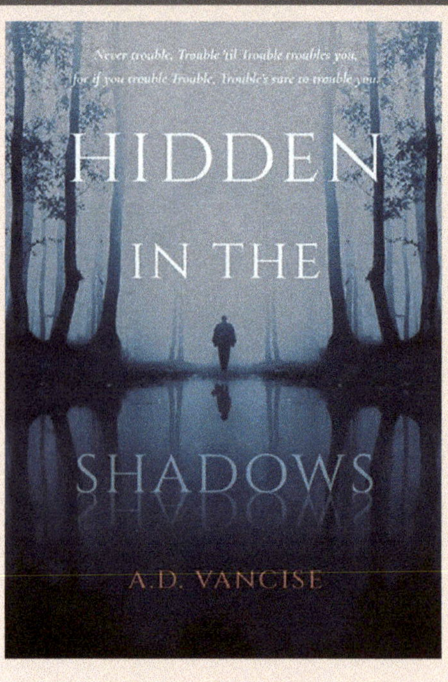

COMING FULL CIRCLE

BY BUDD TİTLOW

A powerful, thought-provoking novel that masterfully blends history, environmental awareness, and human resilience—both captivating and deeply inspiring.

Budd Titlow and Mariah Tinger deliver a compelling conclusion to their *Coming Full Circle* trilogy, a thought-provoking narrative that intertwines history, environmental consciousness, and the resilience of the human spirit. This final instalment builds upon the themes explored in the previous volumes, guiding readers through pivotal moments in American history while confronting the urgent question: can we learn from the past before it's too late?

Titlow, a wildlife biologist and wetlands scientist, brings his expertise to the forefront, crafting a narrative that is both educational and emotionally resonant. The novel follows a diverse set of characters whose stories reflect the evolving relationship between humans and nature. Their struggles and triumphs highlight the environmental and social issues that have shaped America, urging readers to reflect on the lessons history offers.

What makes *Coming Full Circle* stand out is its ability to blend fiction with pressing real-world concerns. The novel is not merely a historical recounting but a call to action, challenging readers to reconsider their role in the planet's future. Titlow and Tinger's storytelling is immersive, with vivid descriptions and well-researched details that bring each era to life.

For those who appreciate environmentally-conscious fiction with a historical and personal dimension, this book is a fitting and satisfying conclusion to an important series. A compelling read that both educates and inspires, *Coming Full Circle* is a timely reminder that history's lessons should not be ignored.

THE FIFTH BRIDE OF PHARAOH

by Catalina DuBois

A beautifully written, emotionally gripping tale of love, sacrifice, and defiance set in a vividly immersive ancient Egyptian world. Captivating and unforgettable!

Catalina DuBois delivers a compelling tale of forbidden love, duty, and defiance in *INFINITY: The Fifth Bride of Pharaoh.* Set against the grandeur of ancient Egypt, this novel blends romance and historical intrigue, drawing readers into the lives of its two star-crossed protagonists.

Sara, a Nubian princess, is bound by duty to become the fifth wife of the all-powerful Pharaoh. However, her heart gravitates towards Matthaios, a foreign slave who sees her as more than just a royal prize. Through richly descriptive prose, DuBois paints a world where power and privilege dictate fates, yet love dares to challenge the established order. Matthaios is a particularly intriguing character, torn between his loyalty as a servant and his growing affections for a woman he cannot claim. His perspective provides an emotional depth that makes their romance both compelling and tragic.

The novel excels in its atmospheric setting, vividly portraying courtly life, rituals, and the constraints placed upon women of the era. While the central romance is deeply engaging, some readers may find the pacing uneven, with moments of swift action followed by slower introspection. Nevertheless, the chemistry between Sara and Matthaios carries the story, making their struggle against societal expectations both poignant and memorable.

For lovers of historical romance, *INFINITY: The Fifth Bride of Pharaoh* offers a captivating escape into a world of passion, sacrifice, and defiance. It is a story that lingers long after the final page, leaving readers to ponder the true cost of love and freedom.

HIDDEN IN THE SHADOWS

by A.D. Vancise

A.D. Vancise masterfully crafts a suspenseful plot filled with atmospheric tension, captivating readers with its intrigue and richly layered narrative.

Hidden in the Shadows by A.D. Vancise is an engrossing mystery that deftly intertwines past and present, weaving a tale of intrigue and suspense in the small town of Woodsville, Arkansas. Evie Day, a 23-year-old who thought she had left Woodsville behind for good, is pulled back by the death of her grandfather. What she anticipated to be a straightforward visit quickly escalates as she uncovers cryptic clues: an enigmatic photograph from 1933, a bizarre vial of blood, and a key to a secret safety deposit box. These discoveries propel Evie into a chilling world, where trusting those closest to her might be her biggest mistake.

This novel effectively builds tension from the outset, drawing readers in with its atmospheric setting and intricate plot. Vancise excels at creating a gripping narrative that keeps readers on edge, eager to unravel the mystery lurking in the shadows. The parallel storyline of Charlie Baker adds depth to the narrative. His journey through suppressed memories of foster care, satanic rituals, and abuse forms a poignant counterpoint to Evie's discoveries, leaving readers wondering how their stories will intersect.

While the novel delivers in terms of suspense, it occasionally lapses into melodrama. Some plot twists, while shocking, feel somewhat predictable, and certain characters could benefit from further development. However, these minor flaws do little to detract from the overall experience.

Hidden in the Shadows is a captivating read for anyone keen on psychological thrillers and dark mysteries. Vancise has succeeded in crafting a novel that not only entertains but also prompts reflection on the hidden horrors that might be lurking in plain sight.

SKULL'S VENGEANCE

BY LİNNEA TANNER

Linnea Tanner delivers a masterful blend of history, fantasy, and drama, creating an unforgettable tale with rich characters and intrigue.

Skull's Vengeance, the gripping fourth instalment in Linnea Tanner's Curse of Clansmen and Kings, masterfully blends historical fiction and fantasy into an enthralling tale of vengeance, power, and sacrifice. Fans of the series will be thrilled by its intricate plotlines and immersive world-building, while newcomers may find themselves quickly drawn into Catrin's epic quest.

Catrin, a Celtic warrior queen, emerges as a formidable heroine, balancing her vulnerability with steely determination. Her journey to defeat her sorcerer half-brother, King Marrock, is fraught with danger, betrayal, and complex alliances. Tanner vividly portrays her struggles, particularly the tension between duty and desire as she rekindles a passion with her Roman husband, Marcellus, amidst the perilous political intrigues of the Julio-Claudian dynasty. Their relationship adds a layer of emotional depth to the narrative, making the stakes feel all the more personal.

Tanner's prose is richly descriptive, seamlessly weaving historical and mythical elements into an evocative tapestry. The use of druids, cursed relics, and dark magic lends a mystical quality to the story, while the brutal realities of war and political manoeuvring keep it grounded. Particularly striking is the imaginative concept of summoning forces through skulls, which adds a fresh and chilling element to the fantasy genre.

While the pace occasionally slows during the intricate world-building, the climactic battles and character-driven drama more than compensate. *Skull's Vengeance* is a satisfying conclusion to the series, appealing to readers who enjoy bold heroines, high-stakes conflicts, and a touch of the supernatural in their historical fiction. Highly recommended for fans of both epic fantasy and ancient history.

SUPER BIG BROTHER

by Deanna Bussadori

Super Big Brother is an enchanting tale that beautifully teaches children empathy and love, making it a must-read for families.

Super Big Brother: New Baby Surprise for Super Big Sister by Deanna Bussadori is a delightful exploration of the emotions that come with becoming an older sibling. Aimed at young children, this beautifully illustrated Kindle edition captures the essence of navigating sibling dynamics through the eyes of Lulu the Little.

The narrative begins with Lulu feeling uncertain and unhappy about the arrival of a new baby. This sentiment is relatable and sets the stage for an important journey of emotional growth. Super Sam, a playful and wise character, guides Lulu in understanding her feelings and teaches her how to embrace her role as a big sister. Through various engaging scenarios, readers witness Lulu learning about kindness, responsibility, and empathy—crucial lessons that resonate with both children and parents alike.

Bussadori's writing is straightforward yet poignant, making it accessible for early readers. The vibrant illustrations by Blueberry Illustrations complement the text beautifully, adding depth and warmth to the story. Moreover, the positive messages about family and love make this book an essential read for families preparing for a new addition.

Super Big Brother offers a perfect blend of fun and education, helping children navigate their feelings in a constructive manner. It earns a well-deserved five-star rating for its heartfelt storytelling and captivating illustrations. This book is sure to be a cherished addition to any child's library, fostering empathy and understanding in the exciting journey of sibling-hood.

A SOUL'S QUEST

by Ketan Kulkarni

A beautifully crafted, soul-stirring fable that inspires self-discovery, inner strength, and living with purpose. Truly uplifting and timeless.

Soar: A Soul's Quest by Ketan Kulkarni is a beautifully written fable that resonates with readers of all ages. At its heart is Soar, a young eagle who embarks on a transformative journey in search of truth, identity, and spiritual purpose. Though the story is framed as a simple quest, it is layered with gentle wisdom and meaningful allegories.

Kulkarni's prose is elegant and evocative, capturing the inner turmoil and quiet strength of his feathered protagonist. The structure of the story—a series of encounters with wise and often mysterious creatures—feels reminiscent of timeless parables. Each interaction serves as a gentle nudge, guiding Soar (and the reader) towards a deeper understanding of what it means to live authentically and with purpose.

What truly sets this book apart is its universal appeal. Children may be drawn to the vivid imagery and animal characters, while adults will appreciate the philosophical undertones and introspective themes. The spiritual elements are handled with care, never veering into preachiness, but offering insight that feels sincere and thought-provoking.

Soar: A Soul's Quest is a quiet triumph—a tale that encourages reflection, inspires courage, and gently reminds us that the answers we seek often lie within. A perfect read for those on a path of personal growth or simply in need of a soul-stirring tale.

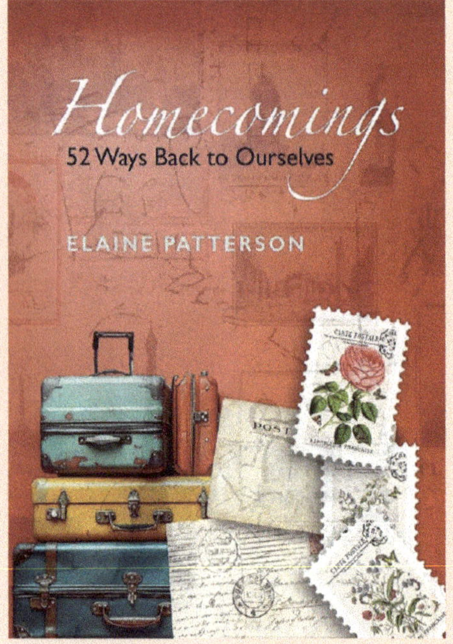

HOMECOMINGS

by Elaine Patterson

A beautifully written, soulful guide that gently leads you home to yourself with wisdom, grace, and heartfelt authenticity.

Elaine Patterson's *Homecomings: 52 Ways Back to Ourselves* is a beautifully crafted and soul-nourishing invitation to reconnect with the self. Written in a deeply reflective and lyrical style, this collection of 52 soliloquies gently encourages readers to pause, breathe, and turn inward amidst the noise of modern life.

Born from journal entries penned during the UK's COVID lockdowns, Patterson's words carry a quiet power—offering solace, insight, and a profound sense of presence. Each reflection is paired with creative invitations and journaling prompts, making this more than a book; it's a companion on a year-long journey of self-discovery and inner restoration.

What sets Homecomings apart is its sincere and heartfelt tone. Rather than prescribe, it invites. Rather than instruct, it opens doors. Whether contemplating solitude, stillness, courage, or compassion, Patterson's prose is both grounding and expansive—holding space for both vulnerability and strength.

There is a poetic rhythm to her writing that makes each entry feel like a warm conversation by the fire—gently guiding us back to the places within we may have forgotten. It's a timely offering in an often disorienting world, reminding us of the profound wisdom that arises when we choose to come home to ourselves.

A tender, wise, and luminous collection, *Homecomings* is ideal for those seeking gentle direction, creative reflection, or simply a reminder that within us all lies a sacred place of belonging.

Highly recommended for heart-led readers, journallers, and seekers alike.

MY PLACE AMONG THEM

by J. Stanion

A powerful, beautifully written novel that captures resilience, identity, and the human cost of forced assimilation with depth and historical authenticity.

J. Stanion's *My Place Among Them* is a powerful and deeply moving historical novel that explores the fraught relationship between identity, survival, and forced assimilation in late 19th-century America. Through the eyes of twelve-year-old John Iron Horse, a Lakota boy who survives the massacre at Wounded Knee, and Carter Heath, a well-intentioned teacher in a government-run boarding school, the novel brings to life the harrowing realities of Native American history.

From the outset, John's resilience and determination are palpable. Thrust into a system designed to erase his heritage—epitomised by the chilling motto "Kill the Indian, save the man"—he struggles to maintain his identity in the face of relentless cultural erasure. Meanwhile, Heath, though initially complicit in the system, begins to question the role he plays in this brutal assimilationist agenda. Their evolving relationship provides the novel with its emotional heart, highlighting the tensions between oppression and compassion, power and resistance.

Stanion's prose is both lyrical and unflinching, rendering the injustices of the time with historical precision while crafting characters that feel heartbreakingly real. The novel does not shy away from the difficult truths of America's past, yet it also offers moments of hope and humanity.

With its well-researched backdrop and compelling narrative, *My Place Among Them* stands out as a must-read for those interested in historical fiction that challenges, educates, and resonates long after the final page. A deserving recipient of multiple literary accolades, it is a story that should not be overlooked.

BOY WANDER

BY JOBERT E. ABUEVA

Powerful, raw, and beautifully written—Boy Wander is a courageous journey of identity, resilience, and self-discovery that deeply resonates.

Jobert E. Abueva's *Boy Wander* is a bold, unflinching memoir that navigates the complexities of identity, ambition, and survival with striking candour. Set against the backdrop of 1970s and 80s Asia and America, this coming-of-age tale traces the extraordinary journey of a young boy living two lives: the celebrated golden child by day and a secret sex worker by night.

From the elite international school halls of Tokyo to the hushed corridors of the Imperial Hotel, Abueva's life is a juxtaposition of brilliance and burden. His achievements—student leader, academic star, athlete—mask a hidden reality that's both heartbreaking and haunting. The tension between societal expectations and his concealed truth is palpable throughout, making the memoir as emotionally resonant as it is revealing.

What elevates *Boy Wander* is Abueva's storytelling—fluid, deeply personal, and remarkably self-aware. His voice matures with each chapter, shifting from youthful deflection to profound reflection. The geographic scope—Manila to Kathmandu, Tokyo to San Francisco—adds rich cultural texture, making his journey feel not only intimate but also global.

While it confronts painful truths, this is ultimately a story of resilience, self-discovery, and quiet triumph. Even decades on, the memoir resonates deeply in today's conversations around identity, acceptance, and the many faces we wear to survive.

Courageous and thought-provoking, *Boy Wander* is an unforgettable read. It's not just a memoir—it's a mirror for anyone who's ever felt the need to hide who they are to be loved.

EDITOR'S CHOICE

THE SPİRE

BY SHAUN GOLDSMİTH

The Spire is a masterfully crafted thriller, combining intrigue, emotional depth, and unexpected twists that keep readers completely engrossed. Highly recommended!

In The Spire, Shaun Goldsmith delivers a gripping and atmospheric thriller that keeps readers on the edge of their seats from start to finish. Set against the backdrop of a luxurious Manhattan skyscraper, the novel opens with the shocking discovery of four brutalised bodies in a penthouse, all linked to the infamous Andrew Levine. Detective 'Diamond' Mike Vogel, a seasoned investigator grappling with his own dark past, finds himself entangled in a web of deception, power, and corruption as he delves into a case that test his limits.

Goldsmith expertly blends elements of mystery, police procedural, and even a touch of roman à clef, creating a multi-layered narrative that is both engaging and thought-provoking. The plot unfolds at a brisk pace, with each twist and turn revealing the complex motivations of the characters involved. Vogel's pursuit of the truth is made even more poignant as he seeks to reconnect with his estranged son, adding an emotional depth to the story that resonates throughout.

The Spire excels in creating a tense atmosphere, heightened by the looming threat of the enigmatic private intelligence company, Talon, adding a chilling sense of urgency to Vogel's investigation. With its sharp dialogue, well-drawn characters, and a plot that keeps readers guessing, The Spire is a remarkable debut that marks Shaun Goldsmith as a noteworthy author in the crime thriller genre. Highly recommended for fans of enthralling mysteries and intricate narratives.

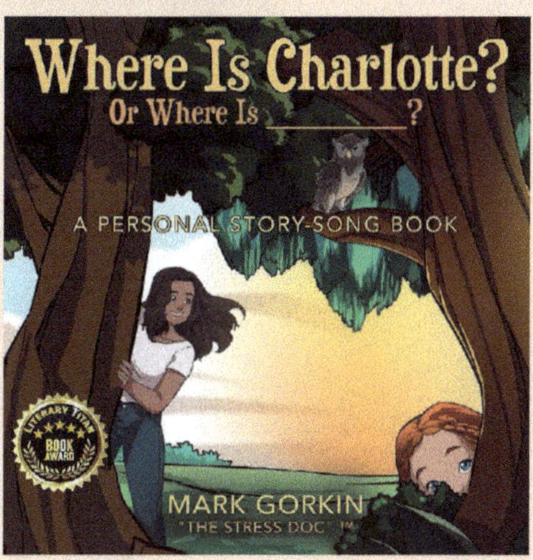

WHERE IS CHARLOTTE

by Mark Gorkin

Joyful, vibrant, and deeply engaging, Where Is Charlotte? celebrates confidence, inclusivity, and adventure through playful storytelling and sing-along charm.

Mark Gorkin's *Where Is Charlotte? Or Where Is _?* is a delightful gem of a children's book that merges playful storytelling with a singable twist. The author blends the timeless charm of "Frère Jacques" with a game of Hide-and-Seek, creating an interactive, musical experience that is as engaging for adults as it is for children. With its lively rhythm and spirited prose, this book is perfect for shared reading and singing.

Charlotte, the dynamic and audacious protagonist, is a firecracker of individuality. Her cheeky and sassy personality leaps off the pages, inviting young readers to embrace their own authenticity and confidence. The book also subtly champions inclusivity through its clever use of changing imagery, allowing children from various backgrounds to see themselves reflected in the narrative. This thoughtful touch adds even more depth to an already well-crafted story.

One of the book's standout qualities is its ability to inspire self-discovery and adventure without losing its warm, connective undertone. Charlotte's escapades are not just about mischief and hiding—they reflect courage, creativity, and an unspoken bond of love, captured beautifully in the author's mantra: "To be your fullest self without being (too) full of yourself!"

In under 40 pages, Gorkin manages to entertain while delivering timeless values. Whether climbing trees or riding the breeze, Charlotte's playful journey will leave every young heart yearning for adventure. For parents and guardians looking to foster both confidence and connection, this book is a delightful pick. Highly recommended!

ENDİNG UNNECESSARY SUFFERİNG

BY PETER RALSTON

Profound, insightful, and transformative—Ending Unnecessary Suffering offers a powerful guide to self-awareness, inner peace, and true mental freedom.

Peter Ralston's *Ending Unnecessary Suffering* is a profound and thought-provoking exploration of the ways in which we create our own distress—and, more importantly, how we can free ourselves from it. Blending philosophy, psychology, and contemplative practice, Ralston offers a refreshing perspective on suffering, challenging the widely held belief that emotional pain is an inevitable part of life.

The book's core argument is both simple and revolutionary: most suffering is not an external reality but a product of our minds. Ralston delves into how thought patterns, assumptions, and ingrained beliefs shape our experiences, often to our detriment. His insights are complemented by practical exercises designed to increase self-awareness and dismantle destructive mental habits. These contemplative practices guide readers toward a greater sense of clarity, peace, and personal empowerment.

One of the book's greatest strengths is its accessibility. While the subject matter is deep, Ralston presents his ideas in a way that is both engaging and comprehensible. He draws on a mix of philosophy and real-world observations, making complex concepts feel tangible and applicable to everyday life.

For those struggling with stress, anxiety, or a sense of incompleteness, *Ending Unnecessary Suffering* offers a compelling roadmap to inner freedom. Rather than providing superficial self-help advice, it encourages genuine transformation, making it an invaluable resource for anyone seeking to cultivate a more peaceful and fulfilling existence. Highly recommended for those ready to challenge their perspectives and take control of their mental well-being.

Celebrating Australian Stories

Claudine Tinellis shares her inspiring journey from lawyer to author and podcaster, championing Australian literature and highlighting the transformative power of creativity, community, and unwavering discipline.

CLAUDINE TINELLIS

INSPIRES THROUGH HER LITERARY JOURNEY AND PODCASTING SUCCESS

"The years I spent as a lawyer taught me the value of discipline."

Literature

BY READER'S HOUSE STAFF

Claudine Tinellis, a former high-flying corporate lawyer turned author and podcaster, stands as a remarkable figure in the literary landscape. With a vibrant career that bridges the structured world of law and the often chaotic world of creative writing, Claudine embodies dedication, imagination, and adaptability. Her story is not only one of reinvention but also a testament to the power of passion and persistence. At Mosaic Digest, we were thrilled to sit down with Claudine to discuss her journey, her insights into the literary world, and her deep commitment to fostering Australian literature through her celebrated podcast, *Talking Aussie Books*.

Claudine's entrance into the world of publishing came in 2014, through an unexpected collaboration that led to her first editorial project. Titled *Coastal Chef: The Culinary Art of Seaweed & Algae in the 21st Century,* the book combined culinary exploration with environmental themes, showcasing Claudine's willingness to delve into unique and underexplored subject matter. But this was only the beginning. Over the next decade, she would carve out a significant space in the literary community, most notably through her podcast, *Talking Aussie Books*. Focused exclusively on Australian authors, the podcast has featured nearly 300 episodes, earning it recognition as one of the top 10 Australian reading and writing podcasts.

Her efforts go beyond amplifying voices; they bring to light the diversity and richness of Australian storytelling. As our conversation with Claudine reveals, her journey highlights the importance of discipline, community, and authenticity in navigating the literary landscape.

The Shift from Law to Literature

For Claudine, the decision to transition from corporate law to writing did not stem solely from a desire to fulfill a creative dream. Practicality also played a role. "Three small children and aging parents forced my hand," she recalls. "I was a senior lawyer in a large Sydney law firm, and at some point, juggling the competing demands became untenable. So I stepped away."

The move may have been a necessity, but it unlocked a new passion that had long simmered beneath the surface. Her collaboration on *Coastal Chef* introduced her to the

> Claudine Tinellis is a beacon of creativity, championing Australian authors and enriching the literary world with passion and innovation.

publishing world, and she quickly fell in love with the creative process. Soon after, Claudine began writing her own stories and actively sought out communities of writers. "I never imagined I would be working in this industry in the capacity I am now," she admits, but her willingness to embrace change and evolve her skill set has allowed her to thrive in a demanding field.

Though she faced challenges, Claudine's legal background proved an asset. "The years I spent as a lawyer taught me the value of discipline, and I've applied this both to my writing and my podcast," she says. "Writing or producing a podcast with consistency and dedication is key. It's a long, sometimes solitary road, but these are qualities I've been able to carry over from my previous career."

Learning from Authors: A Podcasting Passion

When Claudine launched *Talking Aussie Books*, it was not only a platform to showcase Australian authors but also a way to learn from them. Each interview offered her a chance to glean new insights and improve her own craft. "Engaging with other Australian authors has been essential in my creative process," she explains.

The journey into podcasting began with a simple observation: there were no podcasts focused solely on Australian authors. "I was interested in learning more about their journeys to publication, and I thought if I was interested, perhaps others would be too." Since then, she has developed deep connections with writers across genres, building a network that not only supports her podcast but also enriches her personal and creative growth.

One of the most significant lessons Claudine has learned from the authors she interviews is that there is no "correct" path to success. "The same way there isn't a singular road to publication, there is no right way to write," she says. "Each writer has to choose what works best for them and their individual circumstances. Learning that has been liberating for me in many ways."

The Unique Voice of Australian Fiction

Claudine's passion for Australian literature shines through in everything she does, and she believes the nation's stories hold a unique place on the global stage. "Much of what is being written at the moment is a celebration of what it means to be Australian," she says. Australian literature, she explains, reflects the country's multifaceted culture and identity. "It explores the diversity of the Australian experience—stories from marginalised communities, women, Indigenous peoples, life on the land, and the many things that shape who we are now."

For Claudine, the themes of Australian fiction resonate on a personal level, particularly historical and crime novels. "As a history and law graduate, I find myself drawn to these genres," she says. "I guess it's no surprise that I write dual-timeline crime stories myself!" This connection underscores how her academic and professional background continues to inform her creative work.

Advice for Aspiring Writers

For those looking to break into the literary world or forge their voices in Australian literature, Claudine has advice grounded in years of hard-earned experience.

"First, find your community," she advises. "The writing life can be a lonely one, but it's rare to encounter a writer who doesn't have the support of other writers around them. A quick look at authors' acknowledgments will show just how vital this support network is." Surrounding yourself with like-minded individuals provides not only encouragement but also invaluable opportunities to grow.

"Second, create a community around yourself by supporting others. Whether through social media, a blog, a podcast, or another outlet, show your support for other authors. It will come back to you in spades when your own book is published."

Finally, Claudine emphasizes the importance of honing one's craft. Writing is not merely an act of inspiration but also one of skill and persistence. "Take courses, listen to advice from other writers, and read—especially in the genre you intend to write in. This will help you find your voice and ensure that you understand the conventions required for your chosen genre."

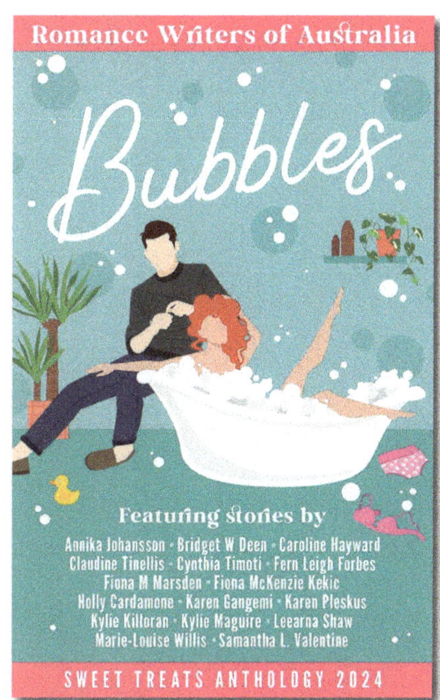

Sweet Treats - Bubbles is a delightful anthology brimming with heartwarming romances. The collection offers sixteen cosy, feel-good stories—featuring second chances, reunions, and first loves—that are perfect for a relaxing binge-read. With charming writing and bubbly charm, it's an ideal escape for romance lovers. Pour a glass and enjoy!

Looking Ahead

Claudine's journey is a work in progress. While she continues to build her podcast and contribute to Australia's literary community, she is also focused on achieving her personal goal of publishing her debut novel. "I have a literary agent now," she says optimistically. "I'm confident my books will find their home in the fullness of time."

Her faith in the process and commitment to perseverance are inspiring reminders to aspiring writers and creatives alike. Claudine Tinellis exemplifies how a blend of discipline, passion, and connection can lead to a fulfilling creative life.

At Mosaic Digest, we are proud to celebrate voices like Claudine's—voices that honour the diversity of storytelling and champion the importance of community and inclusivity in literature. She reminds us all that the road to creative fulfillment may not always be easy, but it is certainly worth it.

Exploring Grief, ADHD And Authentic Narratives

JACLYN PAUL

Writes Compelling Stories and Practical Guides That Bridge Fiction, Advocacy and Life

BY READER'S HOUSE STAFF

Jaclyn Paul, writing as Lena George, stands out as a modern literary powerhouse, skillfully navigating the worlds of fiction and non-fiction. Under her pseudonym, Lena George, she crafts stories that weave queer and neurodivergent characters into compelling narratives, most notably in her 2023 debut novel, She's Not Home. This poignant exploration of grief and family relationships captures the emotional intricacies of its characters, resonating deeply with readers and becoming a book club favorite.

Beyond her contributions to fiction, Paul is a tireless advocate for adults with ADHD. Her non-fiction bestseller, Order from Chaos: The Everyday Grind of Staying Organized with Adult ADHD, offers practical, relatable advice drawn from her own life. Hailed by readers and experts alike, including ADHD authority Kathleen Nadeau, Ph.D., the book is now a cornerstone resource for adults navigating ADHD. At Mosaic Digest, we were thrilled to talk with this multitalented author about her creative processes, personal experiences, and impact as an advocate.

sTransforming Personal Struggles into Support

Order from Chaos earned its spot on numerous "best of" lists for its realistic, empowering approach to managing ADHD. For Paul, the journey to creating it was deeply personal.

"When I started writing about life as an adult woman with ADHD, there were only a few of us out there," she reflects. "Before becoming an author, I worked in human resources and non-profit administration, so I'd already drifted toward supporting people and helping them do their best work. But when you have ADHD, the standard advice for organizing your life often falls short. I wanted to distill what I'd learned and how I'd succeeded, emphasizing the importance of self-acceptance and self-knowledge in the organizing process. Everything has to happen through an ADHD lens."

This focus on self-acceptance has resonated strongly with adults seeking to reconcile their ADHD symptoms with the demands of daily life. Paul's writing isn't about perfect routines but practical systems that reflect reality—a hallmark of her authenticity that readers value deeply.

From Heartbreak to Fictional Truth

In her debut novel, She's Not Home, Paul draws from profound personal experiences to create a deeply emotional story. The novel explores grief and family dynamics while anchoring the narrative in a fictionalized version of her hometown.

"I rarely set out to tackle specific issues in fiction," she says. "My stories begin as a single spark, a seed of an idea that might come from an interaction with a neighbor or something I've experienced or read about." That spark was ignited here by personal tragedy. "I lost a friend to a car accident when we were seventeen. There was this tension between the beautiful landscape we grew up in and that landscape's inherent dangers. I also have a younger sister who always looked up to me when she was small. At some point I thought, it could've been me in that car just as easily as my friend. That would've changed the entire shape of my sister's life."

> Jaclyn Paul, known as Lena George in fiction, delivers heartfelt novels and ADHD resources, balancing advocacy and creativity while inspiring readers with authenticity, practicality, and connection across diverse, meaningful themes.

Though grounded in her own experience, the characters and events of She's Not Home are entirely fictional. The process, she elaborates, was less about dissecting grief and more about storytelling. "The setting is a love letter to that home, but also a meditation on some of the darker aspects of what it means to grow up there."

Creativity With a Clock

Balancing her roles as an author, advocate, and mother isn't without its challenges—particularly as someone with ADHD. Yet Paul's honesty about the difficulties, as well as her approach to managing them, underscores her relatability.

"I don't think ADHD enhances my creative processes," she admits. "When my ADHD symptoms are more present, my creative life suffers. I also spend more time and energy on the basic stuff of adult life because I have ADHD, and this leaves less for creative work."

However, she credits parenthood for helping her develop a sense of focus. "Parenthood has made me who I am, but it also places a premium on my time, which is both motivating and overwhelming. When my son was small, I would schedule multi-day writing retreats to make progress on large projects." This balancing act is made possible by a supportive family. "My husband is so proud of what I've accomplished and is always happy to help make space when I need it."

Building Connections One Post at a Time

In addition to her books, Paul has built an online community through her blog, The ADHD Homestead, which she launched in 2014. "Early on, the blog let me play around with my writing tone and style and see what topics resonated with my audience," she explains. Over time, the blog also helped her grow as a writer and connect with the ADHD community.

The highlight? Reader responses. "Readers write to thank me for articulating a life experience they thought they were enduring alone. They feel I've captured what they couldn't have expressed themselves. That impact and connection is truly an honor."

A Writer Among Writers

Paul also fosters creativity within her local community through Red Pen Addicts Anonymous, a Baltimore-based writers' group she founded. The group's tongue-in-cheek name belies its serious commitment to craft.

"I have a degree in fine arts, and several

years removed from college, I missed those rigorous art-school critiques," she says. The group's earliest months were pivotal. After an initial high turnout, membership dwindled, and Paul worried it was falling apart. "Then I realized everyone is looking for something different, and whoever remained would be the writers looking for the same thing I was. All I had to do was stay true to my original intentions."

Ten years later, Red Pen Addicts Anonymous continues to thrive, proving how a strong creative community can fuel growth.

A Legacy of Connection and Authenticity

Through her work as Lena George and Jaclyn Paul, this versatile author has given readers more than just novels and self-help resources—she has provided connection, understanding, and courage. Whether writing about grief, family, or the challenges of living with ADHD, Paul's commitment to authenticity shines.

Her work offers solace and strength, proving that words have the power to bridge worlds, reshape lives, and remind us we're not alone in our journeys. For Paul, the beauty of storytelling lies in its ability to leave a lasting mark. And judging by her achievements, that mark is indelible.

Jaclyn Paul crafts deeply empathetic stories and life-changing ADHD resources, blending storytelling and advocacy with unmatched authenticity and impact.

SKYLER COLE PHOTOGRAPHY

I rarely set out to tackle specific issues in fiction. My stories begin as a single spark, a seed of an idea."

Jaclyn Paul

A Journey Of Hope, Healing, And Second Chances

ASHLEY WESTON

Shares Her Life, Faith, And The Inspiration Behind Her Heartfelt Novels

BY READER'S HOUSE STAFF

Ashley Weston is a storyteller whose words resonate deeply, offering her readers a unique blend of emotional authenticity, hope, and healing. As an author who has turned her childhood dreams of writing into a celebrated career, Weston crafts narratives that are as heartfelt as they are inspiring. Her ability to address universally profound themes—be it personal growth, forgiveness, faith, or second chances—is beautifully showcased in the much-loved *Marlow's Boys Ranch* series, where the dynamics of found families meet the healing power of nature. Born from her own personal experiences and summers spent in the serene beauty of Colorado, these stories have captured the imaginations of readers across all walks of life.

Weston's work stands apart not only for its evocative storytelling but also for the incredible emotional depth drawn from her life, particularly her journey with chronic illness. Her commitment to making others feel seen and understood is evident on every page, and it's no wonder that her novels have touched the hearts of so many, particularly those who have sought solace and validation through her words. Balancing a bustling family life with her passion for writing, she weaves a spirit of love, faith, and resilience into each of her characters, offering a sense of connection that feels as real as it is uplifting.

As someone who writes with unflinching honesty, Weston reminds us all that pain can serve a purpose and that hope and faith can turn life's struggles into beautiful stories. This interview highlights not only her remarkable insights as an author but also her unwavering desire to remind readers that, even in their hardest moments, they are never truly alone. It is an honour to share her thoughts and wisdom with you in this issue of Reader's House.

Your novels often explore themes of healing and personal growth. How have your own experiences with chronic illness influenced the emotional depth and authenticity of your storytelling?

Dealing with constant pain starting as a young child is not the easiest thing to navigate. I used to spend a lot of time alone and one of the ways I would cope with that loneliness would be to write. Journal my thoughts and feelings, and eventually that turned into story-telling. For me, it's so important to help others feel seen and to know they aren't alone as I was for so many years. If I could portray that in any small way into my stories, I feel like I've done my job, and maybe there's a bigger reason as to why I suffered with it than just for me.

In your "Marlow's Boys Ranch" series, you delve into the dynamics of found families and second chances. What inspired you to set these narratives in a ranch setting, and how does this environment enhance the stories you aim to tell?

Growing up I spent every summer at my grandma's cousin's cabin in Colorado on land. Everything written in my series is based on real people and a real place. I've always wanted to influence youth and help them feel a little less alone in the world, and by creating a safe place for them that struggle, that was important to me. This ranch, though fictional in a sense of being a boy's ranch for healing, was based on a place I often found healing in for myself. Being outside is grounding and healing. Seeing the same two elderly family members who brought a consistent love and kindness to me each summer was so important for how I viewed the external world. Nature and family in a consistent manner is quite powerful to an adolescent.

I also believe in the power of forgiveness, and second chances is a perfect way to relay that in this type of setting. If we can forgive others for "doing wrong", we can also forgive ourselves. It's an ever evolving cycle.

> Ashley Weston opens up about her writing journey, personal struggles, and how faith inspires her compelling novels filled with emotional depth and hope.

Balancing a writing career with motherhood to four children is no small feat. Can you share how your family life shapes your writing process and the themes you choose to explore in your books?

I'm very blessed to have a supportive husband who, if I ask, gives me time to write. But I honestly try my best to show up for my family, they come first, so I tend to write during nap times or after bedtime when they don't need me. I don't want to miss out on their growth. I hope to write stories, though romance infused, with hope and healing to be an example to my children. If we can help our children be better adults, the world will be a better place.

Faith appears to be a significant aspect of your life. How does your spirituality influence the characters you create and the moral dilemmas they face within your stories?

This one is a little more tricky because it tends to be where a lot of opinions arise in readership. Some people love faith-based stories and some don't. I try my best to not focus solely on one aspect of faith to make it more multidimensional with other's beliefs but at the end of the day, my faith is who I am and a part of me, and that will trickle into my stories. With faith comes hope, and with hope anything is possible. Isn't that what we all want? Happy endings and the possibility that anything can happen?

I want to portray real life scenarios of people who struggle, but with the aspect that faith and/or hope helps us to fight through the struggle. Not just suffer through it.

With all of that, there is always a sense of right and wrong, and a moral compass to my characters. I think we are mostly born with those instincts and I want to remind others that once again, they are not alone in those feelings. It's okay to feel a pull, and to make decisions with consequences attached. Good

or bad.

You've mentioned a desire to help readers feel less alone through your writing. Could you discuss a particular reader interaction or feedback that affirmed this mission and perhaps influenced your subsequent work?

I honestly worried that no one would care to read this book because it isn't the normal storyline with tropes and banter. But I've had several women with chronic illness, or with someone they know who has suffered from it, reach out to me and tell me how much they appreciated me being vulnerable enough to write this story. How it helped them to feel understood. How it gave them a chance to feel like the leading role in a story. To me, that is EVERYTHING. That is what keeps me writing.

> *It's so important to help others feel seen and know they aren't alone as I was for so many years."*
>
> **Ashley Weston**

Celebrated Author Discusses Her Creative Journey

JANE DOUCET

Weaves Laughter and Insight into the Heart of Her Nova Scotia Novels

BY READER'S HOUSE STAFF

Jane Doucet is a literary force to be reckoned with. A dynamic writer hailing from Halifax, Nova Scotia, she has managed to carve out a remarkable career that spans both journalism and fiction. From her engaging, award-nominated debut *The Pregnant Pause* to the hilarious yet heartfelt *Fishnets & Fantasies*, Doucet has demonstrated with each work an extraordinary ability to delve into the complexities of human relationships, ageing, and identity, while skilfully wrapping it all in wit and charm. This autumn, she gifts readers the eagerly awaited *Lost & Found in Lunenburg*, promising yet another triumph. A masterful storyteller, Doucet has become renowned for her warm, insightful, and deeply authentic narratives, and her growing legion of fans are sure to be enthralled anew as beloved protagonist Rose Ainsworth returns for another chapter of life — one rife with love, loss, and second chances.

Doucet's tales are undeniably enriched by their distinctly Nova Scotian backdrop, a location she paints with such care and vibrancy that it almost breathes as a character itself. What sets Doucet apart is more than just an ability to transport her readers to another place; it's her uncanny knack for balancing weighty, universal themes — grief, motherhood, intimacy, ambition — with a humour and lightness that leaves readers laughing as much as reflecting. Her work transcends stereotypes, particularly regarding women and ageing, presenting characters who leap from the page with all the complexity, ambition, and vitality that real life affords. Doucet has proven, time and again, that life doesn't mellow with age but rather grows richer, deeper, and endlessly intriguing.

In this issue, we had the absolute privilege of talking with Jane Doucet to discuss her creative evolution, her inspiration, and what readers can expect next as she dips her pen into the world of contemporary mystery. Insightful, candid, and brimming with her trademark humour, Doucet opens the door to her craft and reveals the heart of her extraordinary journey as one of Canada's rising literary stars.

Lost & Found in Lunenburg marks your third novel and revisits the beloved character Rose Ainsworth. What inspired you to bring her back, and how has she evolved since The Pregnant Pause?

In The Pregnant Pause, Rose was turning thirty-seven and tormenting herself (and those around her!) trying to decide whether to have a baby. I wrote the first draft of that novel when I was in my mid-thirties, and it was inspired by my own experiences of motherhood indecision at that time in my life. I started writing Lost & Found in Lunenburg when I was fifty, after a romantic breakup. So, I decided to explore midlife love, loss, and new beginnings with fifty-year-old Rose in that novel. I hope readers will notice the ways in which Rose has matured over those thirteen years.

Your transition from seasoned journalist to acclaimed novelist was sparked by not finding the kind of book you wanted to read. What were the biggest surprises you encountered in shifting from fact-based writing to fiction?

I would say less of a surprise and more of a delight, in terms of being able to stretch my imagination to limits I didn't think were possible. I'm very lucky to have an editor, Whitney Moran, who is a dream collaborator at Nimbus Publishing's fiction imprint, Vagrant Press. Her suggestions for enhancing characters and plot are incredibly insightful. If I hit a creative closed door during revisions, I know Whitney will be there to help walk me through it.

> Jane Doucet discusses her evolution from journalist to novelist, exploring themes of love, loss, and ageing in her Nova Scotian novels, culminating in her latest work, Lost & Found in Lunenburg.

Many readers have praised the balance you strike between humour and serious topics like grief, aging, and sex. How do you find that sweet spot where a story remains both light-hearted and deeply resonant?

That's a great question! There's no secret sauce. I guess it stems from my own sense of humour, and how I view the world. Having a sense of humour helps me process ordinary, sad things that happen — a divorce, the death of a parent, the end of a friendship or a job. Also, I love reading novels with quirky, funny characters, such as Dear Mrs. Bird, Bridget Jones's Diary, and Janet Evanovich's Stephanie Plum series. It follows, then, that I would want to write the same kind of books that I love to read. Writing humour is hard, but also loads of fun.

The setting of your books — particularly Lunenburg — plays almost like another character. What role does place play in your storytelling, and what do you hear from local readers about seeing their community in your fiction?

I was a first-time author with The Pregnant Pause, and I didn't realize that I could showcase setting. For that novel, I didn't take a single fiction-writing workshop; I just winged it and wrote. When I was midway through writing Fishnets & Fantasies, which is set in the tiny coastal community of Lunenburg, Nova Scotia, on Canada's East Coast, I decided to take my first fiction workshop. The instructor said, "Weather is setting." That hadn't occurred to me, and Nova Scotia gets hit by hurricanes and tropical storms. So, in addition to describing the geographic landscape of Lunenburg, which is stunning, I tossed in a storm. I can tell you that local readers adore real details of places they know and love. But you'd better get them right! I live in Halifax, an hour's drive from Lunenburg, and I did a lot of in-person research there.

Your novels feature dynamic older protagonists living fully — including exploring sexuality and ambition. Was this a conscious challenge to stereotypes about aging, especially in women?

Yes and no. I tend to write my novels with protagonists who are my age, which means I'm writing about experiences I'm having, or that my friends and family are having. So while I never say to myself, "I'm going to challenge stereotypes" before I start writing, I seem to end up doing so. I'm a proud feminist, so I'm thrilled when readers tell me they love reading about older female characters who don't just sit around tatting doilies and doing crosswords. Not that there's anything wrong with that, but at almost fifty-seven, I'm still working as a freelance journalist, writing novels, caring for a senior dog, attending exercise classes, in a loving partnership with my husband, looking forward to my stepdaughter's upcoming wedding — life doesn't stop at fifty, or sixty, or at all, if you're healthy and you don't want it to.

Writing a third novel brings both experience and expectation. How did the creative process for Lost & Found in Lunenburg differ from your first two books?

There's more pressure to be successful, certainly. I self-published The Pregnant Pause in 2017, and that was a tremendous learning curve. I wore

Jane Doucet, celebrated Nova Scotian author, shares her journey from journalism to writing acclaimed, heartwarming novels.

many hats: writer, publisher, project manager, event organizer. I hired a small editorial team: editor, designer, proofreader, launch publicist. It was an enormous amount of work, and I had a full-time communications job so I did it all in my spare time. With self-publishing, the main pressure is what you put on yourself. When you have a traditional publisher, as I now do, you want your books to sell well to help their bottom line. With each novel, I've gained more experience, so dare I say my first drafts have gotten better? You'd have to ask my editor!

With your background in journalism, do you find that your reporting instincts still shape your fiction — whether in research, dialogue, or character development?

For research, absolutely. For Fishnets & Fantasies, I interviewed the owner of a small-town sex shop and a waitress, since I had never owned a business or waitressed. Many of the details they gave me made it into the story. Even though it's a novel, I want my characters to be believable. For Lost & Found in Lunenburg, I read several memoirs written by widows. As for dialogue, my characters speak to me, and their voices and thoughts just pop into my head.

You've described yourself as a "lone wolf" when it comes to writing, yet you praise the Writers' Federation of Nova Scotia as your tribe. How have those connections shaped your career as a novelist?

I'm a lone wolf in that I've never been part of a writing group. But I have taken a few writing workshops through the Writers' Federation of Nova Scotia, and I've taught a few, too. I've made wonderful friends through that organization. But I write alone, and I don't share a work in progress with anyone but my editor.

You're currently working on a contemporary mystery — a new genre for you. What can readers expect from this project, and how do you approach writing something outside your usual style?

Readers can expect more of my same humour and heartwarming, quirky characters — but with a twist: murder! I've been reading mysteries since I was young; Nancy Drew was my first foray into that genre. Then I read my mother's Agatha Christie books. I adore Richard Osman's The Thursday Murder Club series, and I've read all of Louise Penny's Three Pines series. As long as the murders aren't gruesome, and there are fun characters and some humour, I'm in. That's what I'm aiming for with Blood Typed, my murder mystery, which Vagrant Press is releasing in May 2026. It has been incredibly hard (red herrings, especially), but so much fun. I'm a pantser, not a plotter, which means I don't have everything worked out when I start writing. In fact, I've waffled on "whodunit" several times! I'm almost done the first draft, so I'd better hurry up and figure it out soon.

> *"There's no secret sauce. I guess it stems from my own sense of humour, and how I view the world."*
>
> **Jane Doucet**

A Candid Conversation on Trauma, Resilience, and Advocacy in Emergency Communications

LEA HARMS

Unveils the Unseen World of 911 Dispatchers in Lives on the Line

BY READER'S HOUSE STAFF

Lea Harms is a voice for the unseen heroes of emergency response, a storyteller who bridges the gap between public perception and the raw reality of life on the dispatch floor. With *Lives on the Line*, her powerful memoir co-written with her sister, she pulls back the curtain on the high-stakes, emotionally charged world of 911 telecommunicators—America's "first–first responders." Her work is a testament to resilience, a tribute to those who bear witness to crisis from the shadows, and a call to action for greater recognition of their vital role.

Harms' background as a retired telecommunicator and her master's degree in communication studies lend her writing a rare authenticity and depth. She doesn't just recount harrowing calls; she dissects the emotional toll, the dark humour, and the unbreakable bonds forged in the dispatch room. Her advocacy, both on the page and in public forums, challenges outdated classifications and champions the mental well-being of her peers.

In this interview, Harms speaks candidly about the weight of selecting stories for *Lives on the Line*, the urgent need for the 911 Saves Act, and the coping mechanisms that sustain dispatchers. Her reflections are as insightful as they are moving, offering readers a profound appreciation for the voices behind the headsets.

Lea Harms' work is more than memoir—it's a lifeline, a validation, and a reminder that every emergency begins with someone who answers the call. Dive into her world, and you'll emerge with a newfound respect for the dispatchers who hold the line between chaos and hope.

Your book describes 911 telecommunicators as "America's First–First Responders." Can you share how that distinction shapes the job's mental and emotional toll compared to other emergency personnel?

Unlike other first responders who go to the field, 911 telecommunicators are dropped into emergencies at the exact moment they unfold—often with no visuals, no physical context, and no opportunity to intervene directly. We rely entirely on our voice, our questions, and our ability to remain calm while someone on the other end is living the worst moment of their life. Many telecommunicators have given CPR instructions, delivered babies, or heard someone's last breaths. That kind of invisible proximity to trauma creates a unique emotional load: you're the first to hear the screams, the silence, or the chaos—but rarely see the outcome or resolution. That lack of closure is one of the hardest aspects to carry.

Being a "first–first responder" means you're the first person to touch that emergency, and your input shapes the entire response. You're absorbing it, triaging it, and rapidly orchestrating help—all while the world still thinks you're "just the person who answers the phone."

> Lea Harms, a former 911 telecommunicator, discusses the emotional toll of dispatch work, the importance of reclassification under the 911 Saves Act, and the power of storytelling in Lives on the Line.

Behind the Headset – With stories ranging from life-or-death situations to moments of unexpected humor, what was the most challenging part of deciding which calls to include in Lives on the Line?

My stories were, without a doubt, a form of therapy. Yet there are still some that live only in my head and heart. I have several that only made it to the draft stage before being pulled—sometimes even before my editor saw them. All of that to say, the most challenging part was balancing truth and emotional responsibility, while also trying not to give the reader secondary trauma. We spent a lot of time organizing the stories so that not too many emotionally heavy moments were placed in a row. Thankfully, my sister and I had collected enough lighthearted stories to space them out appropriately.

Ultimately, we chose the ones that stuck with us long after our shifts ended—good and bad. The ones we still think about while brushing our teeth or tucking our kids in. Those are the stories that shaped who we are, and we believed they deserved to be heard.

The 911 Saves Act aims to reclassify 911 professionals as first responders. How do you think this change could impact the profession, both in terms of public perception and tangible benefits for dispatchers?

Reclassification is a long-overdue recognition of the skill, stress, and split-second decision-making required in this profession. Right now, 911 professionals are federally categorized as clerical workers. That's not only inaccurate—it's damaging. It impacts funding, mental health support, retirement benefits, and more. But even beyond logistics, reclassification would validate something dispatchers have always known: we are essential to the emergency response chain.

I believe the 911 Saves Act will help reshape public understanding, attract more qualified professionals to the field, and give telecommunicators the respect, support, and protections they've earned a hundred times over.

Your book includes a caution about its intense content and the emotional weight of dispatch work. What coping strategies or support systems do you believe are essential for 911 telecommunicators?

First and foremost: peer support. No one understands a dispatcher's experience like another dispatcher. Whether it's a debrief over coffee, a dark joke only your shift partner will get, a game of cards mid-call, or a quiet nod across the console—those shared moments save us.

I also strongly believe in access to professional mental health services—especially therapists trained in trauma and first responder psychology. Beyond that, healthy rituals matter: walking the dog, journaling, faith walks, swimming laps, or making pancakes on your day off. Anything that helps you

Author and advocate Lea Harms, co-author of Lives on the Line, shares powerful insights from her years as a 911 telecommunicator.

return to your whole self.

And finally, knowing when to step away. Whether it's for five minutes or forever, walking away from the console doesn't make you weak. It means you're human.

Many people don't fully understand what happens behind the scenes of a 911 call. What do you hope readers take away from Lives on the Line—both about the profession and the people behind the voices?

I hope readers finish this book with a deeper respect for the invisible backbone of emergency services. Dispatchers are trained, tenacious, and deeply compassionate. We are also flawed, funny, resilient—and so very tired.

I want people to know that behind every call they hear on the news, there's someone in a dark room who picked up the phone and said, "911, where's your emergency?" And they didn't hang up until they knew help was on the way.

If nothing else, I hope Lives on the Line reminds people that there is a voice behind that headset who cares deeply—often anonymously, always completely.

What inspired you and your sister to write Lives on the Line, and what was the writing process like?

After witnessing the weird, the heartbreaking, the absurd, and the downright unbelievable, we always joked that we should write a book. Years of decompressing through late-night texts and voice memos made us realize these stories couldn't just live in our memories—they deserved to be heard. Writing became a way to process, preserve, and advocate. It was both healing and hard—especially reliving certain calls—but having each other to co-write made it a shared act of strength and sisterhood.

What was it like writing this book with your sister?

There's actually an entire chapter devoted to our sisterhood and friendship. Yes—it's wholly uncommon to have two family members in emergency services, especially in dispatch. In a way, it bonded us through shared experiences that would've been completely unattainable for our otherwise polar opposite personalities.

You don't get to choose your family—but when your family chooses the same profession, there's an unspoken camaraderie, a twinning of souls. Writing this book together gave us a rare kind of connection: part therapy, part tribute, and all heart.

What advice would you give to someone considering a career in emergency communications?

Know that it's not just a job—it's a calling. You need grit, heart, and the ability to keep going when no one sees what you're carrying. But also know this: some of your proudest moments will happen behind a headset. And you'll never forget the lives you touched, even if they never know your name.

> “*We are the first to hear the screams, the silence, or the chaos—but rarely see the outcome. That lack of closure is one of the hardest aspects to carry.*”
>
> **Lea Harms**

A Mother's Love, A Writer's Mission, and the Power of Representation

JANNESY DELEON

Champions Inclusion Through Heartfelt Stories Inspired by Her Children

BY READER'S HOUSE STAFF

Jannesy DeLeon is not just an author—she is a storyteller with a mission, a mother with an unshakable love for her children, and a voice for those too often left unheard. Her books, born from personal experience and profound dedication, are more than stories; they are bridges to understanding, empathy, and true inclusion.

Inspired by her children, Gabriella and Nicholas, Jannesy's work shines a light on the beauty, resilience, and joy of children with disabilities, ensuring they are not just seen but celebrated. Her debut book, Tag! You're It, A Story on Inclusion with Gabby & Nicky, is a heartfelt invitation to young readers and families to embrace differences with kindness and curiosity. It's a narrative where disability is not a limitation but a natural part of life's rich tapestry.

Jannesy DeLeon writes inclusive children's books inspired by her disabled kids, advocating for representation and empathy. She balances caregiving with storytelling, proving disability is part of life's beauty.

Balancing the demands of caregiving with her writing, Jannesy's journey is a testament to perseverance and purpose. Her stories are crafted in stolen moments, yet each word carries the weight of her advocacy—proving that representation matters, not as an afterthought, but as a cornerstone of children's literature.

As she prepares to release Here Comes Sam, a touching tale inspired by her family's beloved rescue dog, and expands her work into interactive workshops and resources, Jannesy continues to redefine what inclusion looks like—both on the page and in practice.

In this interview, she shares the heart behind her stories, the challenges and triumphs of her writing process, and her vision for a world where every child feels valued. Her words are a reminder that storytelling can be a powerful force for change—one book, one conversation, one child at a time.

We are honoured to feature Jannesy DeLeon in this issue, and we hope her message inspires you as deeply as it has inspired us.

Your books are inspired by your children, Gabriella and Nicholas, and aim to promote inclusion for children with special needs. Could you share how your personal experiences influenced the themes and characters in your stories?

My journey as an author is inseparable from my journey as a mother and full-time caregiver. Gabriella and Nicholas, my two incredible children, are the heart behind every story I write. They're both non-verbal, non-ambulatory, and live with complex medical conditions, yet their spirits, humor, and resilience shine brighter than words can describe. As their full-time caregiver, I've seen firsthand how often kids like mine are left out, not just from books and classrooms, but from everyday conversations. Sadly, I also realized early on that they rarely show up in picture books—certainly not as central characters with depth and joy. I wanted to change that narrative. My stories are a way to show their world—their joy, their personalities, their value—to families and children who may not otherwise see it. It's an intentional invitation for readers to understand that disability is not something to pity. It's simply part of the human experience. Gabby and Nicky may need support, but they're full of life and deserve to be celebrated.

"Tag! You're It" introduces readers to Gabby and Nicky in a narrative emphasizing inclusion. What message do you hope young readers and their families take away from this story?

I hope families walk away understanding that inclusion isn't a complicated concept. It's about creating space where everyone feels like they belong. Tag! You're It isn't just about disability; it's about friendship, empathy, and recognizing the value in people who may move, speak, or think differently. I want young readers to feel empowered to ask questions, be curious, and lead with compassion. And for families who have children with disabilities, I want them to feel seen—really seen. Because representation isn't just about being visible; it's about being valued.

Balancing writing with raising two children with complex medical needs must present unique challenges. How do you manage your writing process alongside your parenting responsibilities?

The truth is, there are stretches where I don't even look at a manuscript for months. My life doesn't always allow it. Between caregiving, managing medical needs, and everything else that comes with our day-to-day, writing often has to take a backseat. Especially recently, with all that's been going on, I've had to constantly shift gears. But when I do get those windows—no matter how small—I hold onto them. I enjoy the creativity, the process of building a story from scratch, and knowing that I'm working toward something that has meaning. Writing this series is about purpose. It's about showing what inclusion looks like and leaving behind something lasting that centers kids like Gabby and Nicky.

Representation is a central theme in your work. How do you envision your books contributing to broader conversations about diversity and inclusion in children's literature?

PHOTO BY ERMELIN PHOTOS

Author and advocate Jannesy DeLeon with her children, Gabriella and Nicholas, the inspiration behind her inclusive stories.

There's been growing momentum around diversity in children's literature, but disability representation still lags far behind. And when it does show up, it's often oversimplified or used as a teaching tool rather than a celebration of a full human life. I want to shift that. In my books, children with disabilities aren't side characters—they are the story. They're joyful, funny,complex, and worthy of being centered. I also hope educators and parents use my books to spark conversations with their kids and students about what true inclusion looks like—not justsaying "everyone's welcome," but showing it in action.

Are there any upcoming projects or future books in the pipeline that continue to explore themes of inclusion and representation? What can readers look forward to next from you?

Yes—there's a lot I'm excited about. I'm currently preparing to publish "Here Comes Sam", a story inspired by our real-life rescue dog who formed an incredible bond with Gabby and Nicky. Sam's presence in our home has been a beautiful, healing force, and I wanted to capture that kind of connection in a story that blends inclusion, friendship, and unconditional love. I'm also working on my fourth manuscript, continuing the series. Beyond the books, I've been expanding the message of inclusion through hands-on tools—like my Inclusion Affirmation Cards and teacher resource guide—that help educators, families, and kids bring these lessons into real-world spaces. I'm also developing a caregiver-focused project to support those navigating this journey without much help. And on top of that, I'm creating an interactive inclusion workshop for children that makes learning about empathy and accessibility fun and meaningful. Everything I do—whether it's a story, a product, or a conversation—comes from the same mission: to make sure no one feels invisible.

> *Gabby and Nicky may need support, but they're full of life and deserve to be celebrated."*

Jannesy DeLeon

A Conversation on Storytelling, Academia and Motherhood

ASHLEY HASTY

Blends Fashion History and Literary Passion in Hasty Book List

BY READER'S HOUSE STAFF

Ashley Hasty is a dynamic force in both the literary and fashion education worlds, seamlessly blending these disciplines into a captivating narrative. As the creator of the acclaimed *Hasty Book List*, she has transformed a simple Instagram hashtag into a trusted literary platform, offering book enthusiasts a curated space for discovery and discussion. With a background in fashion history, Ashley brings a unique depth to her work, particularly in her historical fiction manuscript set in the 1940s fashion scene. Her ability to weave cultural narratives into storytelling highlights her multifaceted expertise and dedication to her craft.

In this feature, we explores Ashley's journey from academia to the digital literary community, her creative process, and how her diverse roles as a writer, educator, and mother intersect to shape her work.

Fashion History Meets Fictio

Ashley's upcoming historical fiction manuscript delves into the world of 1940s fashion, a period marked by wartime constraints and sartorial innovation. Her academic background in fashion history allows her to infuse authenticity into her storytelling.

"Fashion is never just about clothing—it reflects culture, identity, and even politics," she explains. "In the 1940s, fabric rationing and silhouette changes influenced daily life. I use these details to inform my characters' struggles and triumphs."

Though she's temporarily paused the project since becoming a stay-at-home mom, Ashley remains passionate about the story. *"It's a tale that needs to be told, and I hope to return to it someday,"* she shares.

From Academia to Literary Curation

Before launching *Hasty Book List*, Ashley taught fashion history and branding at Indiana University. This experience profoundly shaped her approach to content creation.

"Teaching taught me the power of storytelling—not just in books but in how people and brands communicate, "she says." I wanted *Hasty Book List to be more than just reviews; it had to be a space where literature, history, and personal experience intersect."*

Her academic rigor also informs her book analyses and interviews, ensuring depth and insight. *"Branding was key to making the platform recognizable and trustworthy,"* she adds.

Ashley Hasty discusses her historical fiction manuscript, the evolution of Hasty Book List, and how her fashion history expertise enriches her literary work while balancing motherhood and creativity.

The Evolution of Hasty Book List

What began as an Instagram hashtag grew into a comprehensive literary resource. Key milestones included launching a dedicated website and attracting attention from authors and publishers.

"Expanding beyond social media let me dive deeper into reviews and interviews," Ashley recalls. "When authors started reaching out, I knew the platform had real value."

Embracing SEO and administrative strategies further solidified Hasty Book List as a go-to destination for readers. *"Once I saw it as a resource rather than just a personal project, everything changed,"* she reflects.

Curating Conversations in the Literary World

As the curator of *Hasty Book List*, Ashley brings a distinctive lens to literary discussions. Her fashion history expertise allows her to explore how cultural narratives shape storytelling, while her teaching background fosters analytical engagement with texts.

"I love connecting books with the right readers and amplifying authors' voices," she says. "Building this community has been incredibly rewarding."

Balancing Creativity and Motherhood

Juggling writing, blogging, teaching, and parenting is no small feat, but Ashley finds synergy in her roles. *"My love for history and storytelling spills into how I engage with my son, whether through reading or museum visits,"* she shares.

Parenthood has also reshaped her creative process. *"I've become more intentional with my time, valuing every moment dedicated to writing or curating."*

Ultimately, Ashley's diverse experiences enrich her work. "These roles make me a more mindful creator and a better storyteller," she says.

A Vision for the Future

Though her historical fiction manuscript is on hold, Ashley remains committed to *Hasty Book List* and its community. *"Literature and fashion are both about expression and identity,"* she reflects. *"I'll keep bridging those worlds, one book at a time."*

For more literary insights and curated book recommendations, visit Hasty Book List https://www.hastybooklist.com) and follow Ashley's journey on Instagram @hastybooklist.

Hasty Book List is thrilled to collaborate with Friend of a Mom, a monthly Chicago dinner series that creates space for moms to connect, recharge, and feel seen. Together, we're launching a new book club designed specifically for Chicago moms—whether you're a devoted reader or just looking to rediscover the joy of reading after motherhood. With thoughtfully selected books, meaningful conversations, and cozy meetups over cocktails and community, this collaboration brings together the heart of Friend of a Mom's supportive gatherings and Hasty Book List's passion for connecting readers.

Ashley Hasty, a dynamic writer and literary influencer, brings history to life through her storytelling and creative endeavors.

Fashion is never just about clothing—it reflects culture, identity, and even politics."

Ashley Hasty

CHARMAINE CHOW

Elevates Modern Skincare With GetHarley's Visionary Blend Of Technology And Expertise

BY LYRA GREEN

Charmaine Chow is nothing short of an extraordinary visionary, redefining the skincare landscape with her brainchild, GetHarley. Armed with a solid foundation in Economics from the prestigious London School of Economics, Charmaine's career trajectory took her from the high-paced world of finance to the nuanced realm of beauty technology. Her professional journey, spanning illustrious firms like Morgan Stanley, KKR, and Goldman Sachs, equipped her with sharp analytical acumen and an innate ability to identify opportunities where others see challenges.

Yet, what sets Charmaine apart is her deeply personal connection to her work. Inspired by her own struggles with skincare and a desire for clarity in an industry riddled with noise, she built GetHarley—a groundbreaking platform bringing science, human expertise, and technology into a seamless, hyper-personalised skincare experience. Guiding consumers to optimal skin health by leveraging a curated network of top-tier practitioners, Charmaine has not only elevated the standard for patient care but also empowered experts to deliver tailored solutions with unparalleled ease.

In this exclusive interview, Charmaine shares her inspiring story, delves into the innovative core of GetHarley, and provides profound insights into entrepreneurship in the competitive health and beauty technology sector. Her forward-thinking approach to sustainability, diversity, and leveraging technology for personalisation exemplifies the responsible yet dynamic leadership needed in today's world. Join us as we explore the vision, grit, and brilliance of the trailblazer behind one of the most exciting developments in modern skincare.

Charmaine Chow shares her entrepreneurial journey, her mission to revolutionise skincare with GetHarley, leveraging AI and human expertise, while championing sustainability, accessibility, diversity, and top-tier personalised care for global consumers.

With the rise of artificial intelligence and technology in skincare, how do you see GetHarley innovating further to improve the customer experience?

At GetHarley we pride ourselves in the ability to make things seamless for the practitioner and the patient at once, so we are leveraging AI to help with automating a lot of tasks and processes in the company to achieve that. That said, we think the ultimate luxury is having a human on the other side of the conversation, so we still want to keep a human-in-the-loop experience at all times.

"I craved a trusted voice to guide me through the thousands of options for my skin."
– Charmaine Chow

GetHarley connects skincare experts with consumers — how do you ensure the quality and reliability of your network of clinicians?

To acquire its network of clinicians, GetHarley actively recruits qualified aesthetic doctors, plastic surgeons, and dermatologists by reaching out to professionals in the field, likely through direct outreach, industry connections, and marketing efforts, allowing users to choose a clinician based on their expertise and availability on the platform, effectively building a large pool of practitioners to match with clients based on their specific skin concerns; users can also choose to be matched with a clinician based on their needs and preferences through the GetHarley platform.

"The ultimate luxury is having a human on the other side of the conversation."
– Charmaine Chow

What challenges did you encounter while raising funds, particularly the recent £40 million, and how did you persuade investors of GetHarley's potential?

In the short run the market is a voting machine, in the long run it is a weighing machine. Fundraising is hard, you have to navigate not only your business trajectory but also adapt to market gyrations. In the early days, people didn't understand the vision of bringing skincare experts into the skin health conversation, investors were mainly investing in a lot of direct-to-consumer brands that were scaling rapidly and marketing-led. So it took speaking to many investors for them to understand that our vision was not to bring more skincare products in to the market but to empower practitioners to help patients find just the right skin solution for them, at all moments of their life.

"Sustainability is something we will always be mindful of and will be strengthened as we grow."

Continued *on page 64*

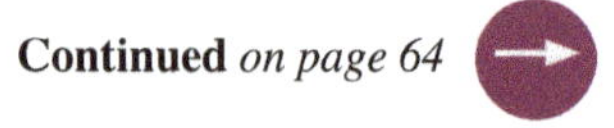

Charmaine Chow, visionary Founder and CEO of GetHarley, championing accessible and personalised skin health through innovation, expertise, and passion.

Continued *from page 62*

PHOTO: *Unlock your best skin yet with GetHarley—a revolutionary platform crafted by visionary Charmaine Chow. Experience seamless skincare consultations that combine expert advice with personalized treatment plans, empowering you to achieve healthier skin with every product curated just for you. Discover the blend of technology and human expertise that sets a new standard in skincare.*

– *Charmaine Chow*

How do you balance promoting medical-grade skincare with keeping the platform accessible to the average consumer?

I think accessibility has many dimensions – information and ease of understanding, as well as price and factoring in your time. I think our practitioners' curation and education of just the right products, for each patient, makes navigating the minefield of information in the industry much easier and much more accessible. In terms of time, you can order products to your door within seconds, again making it more accessible and easier for the consumer. in terms of cost, actually if you invest in 3-5 good quality products and use them to the very last drop, we find that in the long run you spend less. Many consumers might purchase cheaper products over the counter, but find that the products don't work, and so it's a wasted purchase and a waste of money. In addition, you can book an online skin consultation for £40 with a skin professional via GetHarley, without having to leave your house. We believe this has made expert advice accessible for many people.

The skincare market is highly competitive — what sets GetHarley apart from other platforms and brands entering this space?

GetHarley is about helping you find the right products for your skin, not selling you products that you don't need. GetHarley is brand agnostic, so not tied to a particular brand, making it democratic for the practitioner to pick just the right products for each patient. We have a community of practitioners that are best in class in what they do and we are humbled by the opportunity to serve them on our platform and help them service their patients on their journeys to happier healthier skin.

As GetHarley expands globally, what strategies are you considering to address the diverse skincare needs of people from varying regions and ethnicities?

We already serve so many regions and ethnicities... all genders, skin types. We have shipped globally to patients for years. Our expansion plans are about building practitioner communities out of the UK, but because we already serve the world, we are set up to facilitate people from all walks of life. Our offering of over 500 skincare brands, means there is a brand and product range for everyone.

What role does sustainability play in your product curation and business operations, and how do you intend to strengthen this focus in the future?

With skincare experts curating the right products for their patients, patients get great results and so use them to the very last drop. There is therefore less waste compared to buying, trying and discarding (which is much of the beauty industry). GetHarley curated product regimes are posted out in eco-friendly, fully recyclable boxes, with minimal packaging and no bubble wrap.

At GetHarley we practise hybrid working, so people minimise their recruit and maximise productively. We work digitally, we don't print anything we don't absolutely have to print and we also donate the products we don't sell to charities.

Sustainability is something we will always be mindful of and will be strengthened as we grow.

How do you see technology shaping the future of skincare personalisation, and what is GetHarley's approach to staying ahead of the curve?

I think technology will play a huge part in shaping the future of the industry and in particular personalisation of skincare. At GetHarley, we leverage our proprietary technology and data to help our practitioners get feedback on what their patients like, dislike and we share benchmarks against the rest of the skincare industry so practitioners can utilise this information during their consultations and the creation of their treatment plans.

What key lessons have you learnt as an entrepreneur in the health and beauty technology sector that you'd like to share with aspiring business owners?

Dig deep and understand if what is compelling them to start a business is strong enough to go through all the hard work, rejections and challenges. I would also ask them to think through the problem they want to solve and whether it is something they are really bothered by, because you really have to be so enchanted by the problems, to come up with great solutions. I'd also say at some point you also really need to let go and play the quarterback role and hire people.

A Story Of Passion, Experimentation And Spiritual Expression

Janice Taylor's evolution into a full-time artist mirrors the vibrancy and depth of her creations. Known for her evocative and interpretive artwork, Janice's pieces are a compelling blend of faith, personal experience, and cultural immersion. Her mixed media explorations—whether through gelli printing, charcoal, painting, or art on unconventional surfaces like teabag paper—are celebrated for their innovative approach. However, what truly sets her apart is the spiritual core of her artistry, driven by a profound commitment to conveying themes of faith and community.

Janice's journey began in the classroom as a high school teacher, where creativity was integral to both her teaching methods and her students' learning experiences. Later, as she transitioned to mission work, she developed training materials and curricula with the same imaginative mindset. This foundation served as a springboard for her artistic journey. "My creative processes have always been at the forefront," she reflects, adding that her subject matter often emerges from personal moments of faith or images drawn from scripture. "Sometimes, I paint from imagination or sketches I've made during travels," she shares, infusing her exploration with spontaneity and depth.

Janice's Christian faith is central to her work as an artist. She describes her art as interpretive, inviting viewers to derive their own meanings. While she has no objection to the term "prophetic art," she prefers the openness of interpretation. This philosophy underpins her practice, particularly when painting live at church services and conferences. "I have no idea at the start what I'll paint or what colors to use—it's a total reliance on God's Spirit," she explains. Her faith has been her primary motivator, anchoring her transition from her headship role in learning and development to full-time artistry.

A hallmark of Janice's style is her willingness to experiment with different mediums and techniques, driven by an innate curiosity. "Art is about having fun," Janice remarks, revealing her process of entering the studio without a clear plan and allowing inspiration to strike. Whether it's experimenting with materials like teabag paper or embracing trending techniques, she views even the missteps as valuable learning experiences. This playful experimentation speaks to the joy and curiosity evident in her work.

Her extensive travels and experiences with international teams have also left an indelible mark on her artistic identity. During her time with Operation Mobilisation's Inspiro Arts Alliance, Janice collaborated with artists across disciplines, from musicians to actors. Challenges, like adapting to mixed media for the first time in Belgium or working alongside seasoned artists in Italy, shaped her confidence and technique. These early forays into public art have since evolved into a hallmark of her practice, enriching her creative output and global perspective.

Transitioning to a full-time art career wasn't without its hurdles. Leaving her structured role in learning and development for the unpredictability of arts ministry required faith and determination. Financial challenges emerged, as did the need to forge partnerships with fellow Christian artists. However, Janice's proactive and motivated nature enabled her to create opportunities both locally and abroad. She recalls poignant moments of connection, such as painting faith-filled images on her windows during lockdown, which resonated with her community. "Children would ask their parents to slow the car to look at the paintings," she recalls, a testimony to how her art became a tool for engagement and compassion.

Even in retirement, Janice continues to inspire. From canal boat outreaches to ongoing invitations for art ministry, her work remains a dynamic blend of faith, creativity, and service. Janice sums it up best: "I guess I'm not retired but re-tyred," she says with a smile—a fitting metaphor for an artist who has built her life around renewal and reinvention.

Janice Taylor Redefines Faith and Creativity Through Her Unique Artistic Journey

Art & Culture

Janice Taylor masterfully combines creativity and faith, captivating audiences with her imaginative artistry and heartfelt dedication to meaningful storytelling.

> *"My creative processes have always been at the forefront in whatever I was involved in."*

Janice Taylor

The Journey of an Inspiring Biotech Leader RIKA TAJIMA Pioneering Precision Medicine at Red Arrow Therapeutics

Rika Tajima discusses her journey from epidemiology to co-founding Red Arrow Therapeutics, emphasizing strategic leadership and innovative nanotechnology in cancer treatment.

BY EDITOR'S DESK | LONDON

Rika Tajima stands at the intersection of cutting-edge nanotechnology and strategic leadership, guiding Red Arrow Therapeutics towards groundbreaking advancements in cancer treatment. Bilingual in English and Japanese, and an expert in corporate strategy and operations, Rika brings a wealth of experience from her diverse background in epidemiology, biostatistics, and global pharma environments. Her pivotal role in the successful M&A and post-merger integration projects showcases her strategic acumen and operational prowess.

Red Arrow Therapeutics, co-founded by Takuya Miyazaki and Horacio Cabral in 2021, aims to revolutionize cancer treatment through innovative drug delivery systems. Horacio's pioneering work on pH-sensitive nanopolymers, designed to deliver potent cancer drugs directly to tumor sites while sparing healthy cells, serves as the foundation of Red Arrow's mission. This vision of precision medicine inspired Takuya to translate this cutting-edge technology from the lab to patient care, forming the core mission of Red Arrow: delivering life-saving treatments with pinpoint accuracy.

Rika's journey from health economics research to co-founding Red Arrow reflects her passion for applying scientific rigor to real-world challenges. Her experience in health technology assessment and real-world data utilization in Japan provided a robust foundation for her transition into the fast-paced world of entrepreneurship. The dynamic environment of startups, characterized by rapid decision-making and resource optimization, captivated her during her tenure at Astellas Pharma, where she witnessed firsthand the impact of nimble, innovative approaches in the biotech sector.

Joining Red Arrow in 2023, Rika's multifaceted role encompasses fundraising, human resources, and clinical study design. Her leadership style emphasizes open communication, team collaboration, and maintaining a delicate balance between scientific innovation and business acumen. Rika fosters a culture of transparency and support, encouraging her team to voice their ideas and concerns, ensuring a cohesive and motivated workforce.

Rika's insights for aspiring entrepreneurs in the biotech and pharmaceutical sectors highlight the importance of recognizing one's strengths and seeking complementary partners. The intricate and highly regulated nature of these industries demands a collaborative approach, leveraging diverse expertise to navigate the complex journey from innovation to market.

In this interview, Rika Tajima delves into the mission of Red Arrow Therapeutics, her transformative career path, and the leadership philosophies that drive her to shape the future of cancer treatment.

What is the mission of Red Arrow Therapeutics? What inspired its founding?

Many known substances have high potential as drugs for cancer which currently cannot be treated, however they often harm healthy cells as side effects while targeting cancer cells. Horacio Cabral, a professor at the University of Tokyo and a world-leading researcher in nanomedicine, invented pH-sensitive nanopolymers that encapsulate such powerful drugs. These polymers form a protective shell around the drug, creating a molecule akin to an egg. When systemically injected, these molecules travel through the body to the target cancer site. The shell protects the healthy organs from the drug's effects. Once at the cancer site, where the pH is lower than the rest of the body, the shell breaks and releases the potent drug. The drug recruits immune cells to the cancer site, working together to destroy the cancer. These eggs act like a nano-sized Trojan horse within your body.

However, transforming cutting-edge technology into patient-ready treatments is a challenging journey. Takuya Miyazaki, who earned his PhD in Horacio's lab, recognized this and was inspired to bridge this gap. He decided to start a company to nurture Horacio's groundbreaking technology as swiftly and efficiently as possible, leveraging resources from around the world. And hence, Red Arrow Therapeutics was co-founded by Takuya and Horacio in 2021, with the mission to save lives by delivering drugs bulls-eye.

Can you share your journey from your early career in health economics research to co-founding Red Arrow Therapeutics? What motivated you to transition into entrepreneurship?

My background is in epidemiology and biostatistics. Applying scientific and strategic thinking to real-world practice and making a tangible difference has always been a driving force for me. I thrive on daily collaborations with dynamic people to tackle new challenges. This led me to explore uncharted territories, such as the initial adoption of Health Technology Assessment in Japan and the use of real-world data in Japanese regulator-required post-marketing safety studies. Through these experiences, I learned to manage stakeholder expectations, influence without authority, and keep teams motivated amid uncertainty.

I was introduced to entrepreneurship while part of the R&D collaboration team between Astellas Pharma and iota Biosciences, a MedTech startup in California. This collaboration eventually led to Astellas acquiring iota.

Witnessing the speed and flexibility of the startup environment compared to big pharma was eye-opening. The process of prioritizing limited resources to find optimal solutions through speedy trial and error was exhilarating.

Around this time, I met Takuya and Horacio. Takuya's quick thinking and enthusiasm, and Horacio's sincerity and ardentness towards his research intrigued me. I admired the technology and felt that my problem-solving skills and a wide spectrum of experience in pharma would be a great addition to the team. Moreover, I wanted to challenge myself in a smaller organization to see if I could make a more significant impact. I now realize that, in a startup, you can, or inevitably end up doing everything, which feels more hands-on. I joined Red Arrow in 2023, contributing as a jack-of-all-trades in areas from fundraising, human resources, to clinical study design, and eventually became a co-founder.

As a co-founder and VP, what have been some of the most significant challenges you've faced in building and growing Red Arrow Therapeutics, and how have you overcome them? How would you describe your leadership style, and how do you foster a positive and productive culture within your team?

I've heard a saying that more than half of biotech failures are a result of operational challenges rather than scientific/technical challenges. One of the most significant challenges has been building and maintaining a strong team. The size and expertise level of the team must be necessary and sufficient at different points in time to remain nimble and financially prudent. The impact of each team member is vast compared to larger organizations. Additionally, startups are high-stress environments: volatile and demanding.

Above all, I try to be a good communicator, especially a good listener. Many leaders are adept at expressing their opinions, but not everyone feels comfortable speaking up towards them. What needs to be said in the best interest of the company may not be the most comfortable. I strive to create an environment where team members feel safe to straight-talk. I also value being open about what I don't know and asking for help in a speedy manner. Having a diverse network of mentors has been invaluable through by startup journey. Additionally, timely communication is crucial.

As a leader, I value maintaining a balanced focus on both the science and the business. Ultimately, a sense of contributing to patients and making the world a better place get me up in the morning, and I aim to share this sense of purpose with the team, fostering pride in our work.

What advice would you give to aspiring entrepreneurs, especially those looking to enter the biotech and pharmaceutical sectors?

Biotech and pharma are unique within the startup space. They are patent-driven, highly regulated, and require years to generate revenue, unlike consumer products. This niche demands a myriad of expertise. No one person can cover every necessary skill. Identify your strengths and weaknesses, find complementary partners, and let's get started!

Rika Tajima, co-founder and VP of Red Arrow Therapeutics, leading the charge in innovative cancer treatments through nanotechnology.

Dr. Shirin Lakhani: Transforming Lives with Expertise, Compassion, and Innovation in Aesthetic Medicine and Intimate Health

DR SHIRIN LAKHANI

Redefines Aesthetic and Intimate Wellness Through Innovation and Advocacy

Dr Shirin Lakhani merges medical expertise with aesthetic innovation, championing intimate health, patient safety, and natural results. She advocates for stricter industry regulations and empowers patients through regenerative treatments like the O Shot and P Shot.

By Reader's House Staff

A visionary in aesthetic and regenerative medicine, Dr Lakhani combines precision, compassion, and advocacy to transform lives and redefine wellness standards.

In an era where conversations about menopause, hormonal health, and intimacy are often shrouded in stigma, Dr. Shirin Lakhani stands as a pioneering force for change. A leading expert in aesthetic and regenerative medicine, Dr. Lakhani combines medical precision with compassionate care to redefine wellness—both inside and out. From groundbreaking treatments like the O Shot and Vampire Facial to her advocacy for stricter industry regulations, she is transforming the way we approach aging, confidence, and intimate health.

A Journey Rooted in Medicine and Innovation

Dr. Lakhani's career began in anesthesia and general practice, but her fascination with regenerative medicine led her to aesthetics. "I wanted to merge medical expertise with artistry," she explains. "Aesthetic medicine isn't just about looking good—it's about feeling empowered, whether through skin rejuvenation or intimate wellness."

Her approach is deeply personalized, emphasizing natural results over dramatic alterations. "The goal is enhancement, not transformation," she says. "Every treatment should align with a patient's unique features and lifestyle."

Championing Regulation and Safety

One of Dr. Lakhani's most passionate causes is tightening regulations in the UK's aesthetics industry, where non-medical practitioners often perform high-risk procedures with minimal training. "Patient safety is non-negotiable," she asserts. "We need legislation ensuring only qualified medical professionals administer injectables and other invasive treatments."

She works closely with the Joint Council for Cosmetic Practitioners (JCCP) to push for reform, advocating for standardized training, safer clinical environments, and better public education. "Patients deserve transparency—knowing their provider's credentials and the risks involved."

Breaking Barriers in Intimate Health

Dr. Lakhani is also a trailblazer in intimate wellness, offering treatments like the O Shot (for women) and P Shot (for men), which use platelet-rich plasma (PRP) to rejuvenate tissue, boost libido, and address issues like vaginal dryness or erectile dysfunction.

Her book on the P Shot was born from a desire to destigmatize men's health. "So many suffer in silence due to embarrassment," she notes. "Regenerative treatments offer a natural, medication-free solution—but first, we need open conversations."

The Future of Aesthetics: Science Meets Holistic Care

Excited by advancements in regenerative medicine, Dr. Lakhani highlights innovations like exosome therapy and biohacking. "The future lies in harnessing the body's healing abilities while integrating lifestyle factors like nutrition and hormone balance," she says.

For those considering aesthetic treatments, her advice is clear: "Research your practitioner thoroughly. Look for medical credentials, before-and-after evidence, and someone who prioritizes your safety and goals."

Empowering Patients Through Education

At the heart of Dr. Lakhani's practice is patient empowerment. "Knowledge is confidence," she says. "I ensure every patient understands their options, risks, and realistic outcomes before making a decision."

Whether through her clinic, media appearances, or advocacy work, Dr. Shirin Lakhani is reshaping the landscape of aesthetic and intimate health—one honest conversation at a time.

SOURCE: Beauty Prime

Reader's House

LONDON'S LITERARY GATEWAY

READERSHOUSE.CO.UK
ISSUE 54
YEAR 2025
GLOBAL EDITION

The Mastermind Behind Award-Winning Horror Novels

JOHN K. ADDIS

Meet The Author Who's Captivating Readers With Haunting Tales And Unforgettable Characters

INTERVIEW

Literary Stars

Writers Who Inspire Change

Alise Lee Goldenberg
Ashley Hasty
Ashley Weston
Autumn M. Birt
C.E. Clayton
Claudine Tinellis
Deepak Gupta
Dianne C. Braley
James Gilbert
Jaclyn Paul
Jane Doucet
Jannesy Delcon
Joan Epp
Joe Clark
Joe Kilgore
Joseph O'donoghue
Lea Harms
Liliana Tommasini
Raz Mihal
Shani T. Night
Stenetta Anthony
Tina Sloan

EDITOR'S CHOICE
Best Books to Dive Into

Available in

PRINT

Americas to Australia

Europe to Africa Reader's House is available over 190 countries and thousands of retaiers, platforms including Amazon, Barnes & Noble, Walmart, Waterstone's .....

ELECTRONIC

It is an electronic (flip book) format and interactive. Accessable from electronic devices like pc, smart phone, notepads..

ONLINE

All interviews, we conduct make them accessable online for free.

SOCIAL MEDIA

We are on Facebook, Instagram and X. Please follow us on social media
@readershousemag

contact us today for an interview opportunity at
editor@readershouse.co.uk

And so much more ...

Key Partnerships and Future Initiatives

Expanding the Boundaries of Authors and Books

Being featured in Reader's House means gaining visibility not just in print edition, but across the entire media spectrum in the US, UK, Europe and beyond

Key Media Partnerships:

- Associated Press (reaching 50%+ of global population)
- Benzinga (5M monthly visitors)
- Nexstar (68% U.S. TV household penetration)
- Major search engines: Google News, Google, Yahoo, Bing, Ask
- EIN Press Wire coverage
- NewYox Media magazines coverage (Mosaic Digest, Reader's House, CEO Vision, Beauty Prime...)

Broadcast & Digital Coverage:

- Major U.S. network affiliates
- 150+ million monthly radio website users
- 500+ UK media outlets
- Minimum 5 to 20 media placements per country (Albania to Zambia)
- Enhanced SEO positioning with quality backlinks from each media
- Optimized presence on e-commerce platforms)

Distribution Highlights:

- Available through major retailers including Amazon, Barnes & Noble, Walmart, Blackwells and Waterstones
- Available through local retailers Alaska to Wisconsin in the United States.
- Available in print LIFETIME
- Featured across 3000+ media platforms in the US, UK, Europe and beyond

contact us today for an interview opportunity at
editor@readershouse.co.uk

www.ingramcontent.com/pod-product-compliance
Lightning Source LLC
Chambersburg PA
CBHW041206100726
47911CB00016B/874

* 9 7 8 1 6 4 2 2 6 4 3 2 6 *